Foreword

This year, the Young Writers' 'Poetry In Motion' competition proudly presents a showcase of the best poetic talent selected from over 40,000 up-and-coming writers nationwide.

Young Writers was established in 1991 to promote the reading and writing of poetry within schools and to the youth of today. Our books nurture and inspire confidence in the ability of young writers and provide a snapshot of poems written in schools and at home by budding poets of the future.

The thought effort, imagination and hard work put into each poem impressed us all and the task of selecting poems was a difficult but nevertheless enjoyable experience.

We hope you are as pleased as we are with the final selection and that you and your family continue to be entertained with *Poetry In Motion London* for many years to come.

£12-99

London
Edited by Allison Dowse

 Young**Writers**

First published in Great Britain in 2004 by:
Young Writers
Remus House
Coltsfoot Drive
Peterborough
PE2 9JX
Telephone: 01733 890066
Website: www.youngwriters.co.uk

SB ISBN 1 84460 398 9

Contents

Connaught School for Girls

Convent of Jesus & Mary Language College

George Mitchell School

Kieran McGarry (11)   89
Nyle Okebu-Stewart (11)   89

Kingsmead School
Jhozette Samuel (14)   90
David Gathard (15)   90
Cassie Robinson (14)   91
Alex Bailey (14)   91
Moses Fapohunda (14)   92
Diana Mutanho (14)   93

La Sainte Union Convent School
Nicola Tozzi (13)   94
Paula O'Dwyer (12)   95
Natasha Otto (11)   96
Sandra Atimokidi (11)   96
Denise Osei-Kuffour (12)   97
Brooklyn Quinn (13)   97
Roisin O'Reilly (17)   98
Ilda Abi-Khalil (12)   98
Rebecca Oduah (12)   99
Sabrina Babo (11)   99
Alison Fernandes (12)   100
Katherine Wise (12)   100
Katy Tobin (12)   101
Jackie Atta-Hayford (11)   102
Rachel Fernandez (12)   103
Hayley Teixeira-Roxburgh (13)   104
Vanessa Gawaran (12)   105

Leyton Sixth Form College
I Mieng Wong (18)   105
Mbalu Saine (17)   106
Abdul Karim Jabbie (17)   107
Bilkis Begum (16)   108
Falon Paris (18)   109
Lorraine Watson (17)   110

Little Ilford School

Sheun Oshinbolu (11)	110
Pardeep Singh Lall (14)	111
Anish Mandalia (14)	111
Asma Bhol (15)	112
Rohima Uddin (11)	112
Nabeeha Khan (11)	113
Rumana Begum (11)	113
Mahvesh Rana Javaid (13)	114
Jahanara Begum (12)	115
Priya Kanabar (14)	116
Sehar Nizami (11)	117
Rukshana Ali (12)	117
Shuhena Bhanu (13)	118
Shahina Khan (13)	119
Jasmine Chowdhuary (11)	119

Newham Sixth Form College

Jodianne Taylor (17)	120

North Bridge House School

Shivani Shah (11)	121
India Browne Wilkinson (11)	121
Moritz Hellmich (11)	122
Venetia Stefanon (14)	123
Daniel McKeever-Crowcroft (10)	124
Julius Judah (11)	124
Oliver Newman (11)	125
Georgia Mackenzie (13)	125
Natalie Mallin (13)	126
Tariq El Gazzar (13)	127
Jonathan Birkett (12)	128
Charlotte Thompson (15)	129
Amaryllis Garland (14)	130
Max Murdy-Flisher (14)	131
Daniel Townsend (14)	132
Lucilla Braune (15)	132
John Shurety (15)	133
Alexander Robertson (15)	134
Darius Anvarzadeh (13)	134
Josh Yentob (15)	135

Ifrah Jeylani (15)	162
Hannah Cadir (15)	163
Ayan Yusuf (11)	163
Ian Barnor (15)	164
Nadifa Ahmed (11)	164
Andrew Larbi (15)	165
Rachel Graver (12)	165
Kenisha Cooke-Weir (13)	166
Jade McElligott (13)	166
William Earles (15)	167
Nicole Phillip (14)	168
Jacqueline Abakah (11)	169
Sivanna Sherry (13)	170
Aydrous Yousef (13)	171
Adolf Bour Jnr (15)	172

Richard Cloudesley Special School
Tasos Kanas (12)	172
Gurkan Bozdere (12)	173
Luke Hutchins (12)	174
Matthew Ellerbeck (13)	175
Sebahat Cinar (14)	176

Sarah Bonnell School
Amandeep Sidhu (11)	176
Luthfa Begum (12)	177
Fahimah Khanom (12)	177
Rachel Roberts (12)	178
Thelma Simpson (12)	178
Beatrice Owusu-Ansah (12)	179
Sophie Dar (12)	179
Senel Akarca (12)	180
Leeacea Robinson (12)	181
Rochelle Rodgers (14)	182
Oluwaseyi Akiwowo (12)	182
Maegan Sayers (11)	183
Lauren Moynihan (12)	184
Lena Ismay (12)	185
Saffya Yaseen (11)	186
Charlie Kaur (15)	186
Syeda Fazaila Hussnain Bukhari (12)	187

The Mount School

The Whitefield Special School & Centre

The Poems

A Day Of Truth

The sky suddenly forms grey clouds, underneath which,
Pupils march to the hall in a solitary, sombre line.
I sit at a desk all straight and tense,
'Are you alright?' one concerned teacher asks,
The corners of my mouth crease into a forced smile.

Destiny awaits us.

'One hour thirty minutes starting now!'
The silence hits you hard - I am too scared to move,
Scanning the paper I ignore my desire to laugh.
My pen rolls onto the floor, the noise echoing.
You can feel the flinch spread across the room.
Patrolling teachers regarding us,
I look up only to receive an evil glare.

I scribble until my hand feels ready to fall off,
A lump develops on my middle finger.
Twenty minutes left - where did it all go?
I feel a sniff coming on
And I have an overwhelming desire to visit the ladies -
Alas, I have no time, so I cross my legs
And inhale deeply; at last I have finished.

All over.

Excitable students discussing answers,
I wince, for I am sure I have failed.
I go outside to seek solitude,
Giving a deep sigh.
I feel so much better already,
I relax. I smile.

The exams are all over -
At least until next year . . .

Lucy George (16)

Happy Now

Are you happy now?
I wonder are you
Happy now?
Now you have used me
Happy now?

With all the lies and deceit
Are you happy now?
Happy now?
We have finished thanks to you
Happy now?

What goes up has to come down
We went up high, now we have fallen
For others
Are you happy now?
Happy now?

Guess you could see I felt something
Now that I have gone
Are you happy now?
Happy now
Are you?
I am wondering

Guess we finished ages ago
Is that good?
I was blind to the fact you loved her
And not me
Are you happy now?
Happy now?

I guess deep down I knew
You and me were no longer
It was you and her
And just me on the side
Are you happy now?
Happy now?

I should've guessed no one has loved me
The way you did
Now you love her more than you could ever love me
She has the privilege
I just have the memories
Are you happy now?
Happy now?
Happy now?
Are you happy now?

Katie Gillett (14)

Autumn

The summer has gone,
The sun has already shone.
Autumn is here,
I feel cold in my ears.

Hallowe'en is coming,
Witches are humming.
Doors are screeching,
Little girls screaming.

Remember the 5th November,
You should remember.
The fire is red,
It will burn right through thread.

The sky is not blue,
Time to put on warm shoes.
The weather is foggy,
The rain is getting my clothes soggy.

The leaves are brown,
They're hitting the ground.
The summer has gone,
Autumn is here.

Rafael Soares (13)

Girl In The Mirror

Pull away her unseen veil and rise to view
If you're closer it's easy to track the tears
Those tears streaking down her face are
Droplets of darkness
Each tear forming has a story and a memory
She cries as her wound doesn't seem to heal
Getting caught in the web of lies
Trying to fill the emptiness
Lost emotions whisper to her and hunting her fears
A piece is gone and the puzzle undone
They tried to kill the pain but was tempted for more
Saying in jealousy you're perfect of nature
As I am seen in self-indulgence
Spend a lifetime chasing life and you end up chasing death
You arrive and set off the fires in Hell
No floors when you're pretending
Nightmares take over my mind
Saying you're numb without a soul
But who can decide what they dream
Her smile is her make-up
Without a mask where will you hide?
Can't hide no more, you're lost in your heart
Lost in mysteries I stare back seeing myself.

Maya Pillai (12)

Angry - Fierce - Deadly . . .

Thunder
Volcano, a deadly murderer at midnight
Volcano, like a bulldozer, a murderous destroyer
Angry - fierce - deadly

Volcano, lava flowing downstream
As thick as blood
Volcano, stretches and stirs . . . *eruption!*
Angry - fierce - deadly
Volcano, a sense of death
Angry - fierce - deadly
Volcano, evil prisoner
Angry - fierce - deadly

Sunshine

Volcano, a stunning scene of life
Volcano, brings joy to people's faces
When they lay eyes on it
Volcano, its rocky dress that flows
Thunder . . .

Nada Abuknesha (14)

The Dove

Draping its wings over its elegant body
It sits upon a leaf-sprouting branch
Laying its eyes upon the pieces of cotton wool
In the everlasting pit of darkness and light

Gently raising each bunch of its feathers
As if it was picking up a bunch of bananas
It takes off like a graceful piece
Of white silk ambling in the wind

Like a neat tumbleweed it travels with the air
Until flopping like a piece of ribbon being
Dropped from the sky and down.

This graceful creature's head like the moon
And its eyes like shimmering ladybirds placed
On the side of its head
It swoops onto a terracotta-tiled rooftop
Like a floating feather

This beautiful creature settles into a small hole in the roof
As the sky colours itself black
After the watery orange paint has gone

The only thing in sight is the moon
And the darkness of the night.

Grace Smith (11)

Gone Again

Someone's waving back at you,
Departing on that train from view,
Rounding smaller down the track,
Are you sure now looking back,
You'll want to leave on this train's track?

That train, it's carrying far away,
The woman that once came to stay
And so, upon this platform I shall stay,
Until that rumbling train one day,
Does bring you back to me to stay.

Our joy shall last until the day,
The train once more takes you away,
Rounding smaller down the track,
This woman once more looking back.

Still taking every lover's look at
The platform where she took that lasting gaze,
Just looking back and moving slowly down the rounding track,
Then silence, empty station, track,
For she's no longer looking back!

Rodger Robinson

Fairy Lights

Her teeth are like glowing pearls
Accompanied with dark blooming curls.
Her smile lights up even the darkest of days,
Giving hope and love to people every single day.

Her eyes outshine the envious sun,
Because compared together the sun looks overdone.
Her cheeks twinkle brighter than the lonely stars,
Even from afar her cheeks are fairer than some.

She has spider-like fingers
And a rabbit-toothed grin.
Her laugh is similar to a hyena's scream
And her ears look like they come from a nightmarish dream.

My sister, who is always true and there for me,
Never gives up on her wildest dreams.

Saskia May Ellis (13)

Concrete

There's no beaches, no sand in this concrete land,
No boats, no yachts, just concrete blocks,
Where man turns sour from the concrete towers,
As the concrete places create concrete faces.
You see, it's straight from the womb into a concrete room.
Now I don't wanna die in this concrete tomb,
But it's hard to stay humble in this concrete jungle.
When life's similar to how the concrete crumbles,
As our concrete vision is our own concrete prison,
Where outta the seat on the concrete street,
Man is roaming till he gets concrete feet,
Now it won't be long till the concrete speaks,
But then nothing's surprising in this concrete horizon,
Ending in a concrete cell with no more than a concrete smell
Welcome to London, welcome to Concrete Hell!

Andy Laas (17)
Ashbourne College

Beacon In The Mist

Walking in a daze
Darkness seeping through my mind
Get away from me!

Flying far away
Being chased and followed far
Beacon in the mist

Cold, misunderstood
Fighting hard but fighting fair
Cold but not alone.

Shaffi Batchelor (12)
Bishop Challoner Catholic Collegiate School

My Mum's Eyes

My mum's eyes are shining like a star,
like a pattern lighting up the sky.
Driving down the road in a red car,
be sure not to give you a fright.

To be grateful and never be leaving,
like sticky glue stuck to paper,
to be sure she won't stop breathing.

My mother's eyes shining the day away,
until every month goes round.
January, February, March, April, May,
Every day she makes a happy sound.

My mum can be happy, my mum can be sad,
My mum can be good, my mum can be evil,
But every day she makes me glad.

Matthew Pert
Burlington Danes School

Our Love Now

I said, 'Observe how the arrows of the
raindrops damage each leaf, but the
sunshine will rise and lift the leaves
towards the light.'

She said, 'Although the rain will pass and
the sunshine raises the leaves, the dents
will always be an everlasting memory.'

I said, 'Observe the virus of the
computer, the work may be gone, but it
can be redone and the virus can be
destroyed, such is our love.'

She said, 'Although the work can be
repaired and the virus wiped out the
computer is different and incomplete,
such is our love now.'

I said, 'When your watch stops you feel
late and the day seems longer, but you can
put the time right before long it is the
same, our time together is such.'

She said, 'After time stopped it doesn't
stop life, during that time differences must
occur the schedule will be different, such
is our love now.'

I said, 'Listen to the sound of the bee,
waiting to attack. The bee is frightening
but it will soon be gone leaving a sting that
is forgotten the breach in us can be fixed.'

She said, 'Although the bee is frightening
when attacking and the sting is no more,
it damaged itself from protection,
the bee is forever asleep,
such is our love.'

Jyoti Kaur Virk (14)
Burlington Danes School

Valentine

Not a red rose or a satin heart
I give you a strawberry
It is a red, heart-shaped fruit
It promises growth
Like the seeds it produces

Here
It will give you love, like the love
We share together
Like a giant juicy strawberry tree
It will never fall because its roots are stuck to the ground
As is my love

I am trying to be truthful
Not a cute card or a kissogram

I give you a strawberry
Its rough outside may fool you but take a bite and
Reveal to yourself the true feel

Take it
Its fresh sweet smell
Will hang around

Lethal
Its juice will stain your heart

That means it will be there forever, always.

Daniel Lewis (13)
Burlington Danes School

Britain

Britain! What does it mean to you?
Trafalgar Square, with its double-decker buses
And its lions that stand proud?
Maybe it is the filthy pigeons
Or the buskers that are loud?

Many foreigners gather there,
Especially for the Haagen-Dazs,
But is it the ice cream that brings them here
Or everything else Britain has?

The Trocadero is always packed,
On Friday night it is the worst,
Bright lights and arcade games,
The drunk men, calling all sorts of names,
So I ask you again what does Britain mean to you?

Fawzia Hasham (13)
Chestnut Grove Visual Arts Specialist College

Moving In . . .

I'm a teenage girl
Moved halfway around this world
Moving in, being welcomed
Waking up in a new environment
People look at me in a different point of view
'She's the new girl,' people say, 'just moved in at number two'
I've seen my picture of who I am
It's kind of funny when you come to think of things
Different in fact getting in touch with my feelings
But you don't know what the future holds
So let me think, I'm moving in . . .

Nikki Matthews (14)
Chestnut Grove Visual Arts Specialist College

Britain

Britain, what do you think?
People out at night showered with drink,
Late night robberies, death everywhere,
Dirty streets, beer-bellied men at home.

Gangs fighting at school,
Smoking, drinking, doing drugs like a fool,
Missing children, Victorian teeth,
Teenagers shoplifting, showing off.

This may be true at night, but . . .

You wake up to morning, GMTV,
Smiling faces, birds singing,
The trees wake up and bloom out nice,
You go to the shop, find out the right price.

Seeing everything nice and bright,
Everything shining, everything light.
Children happy running round and round,
Jumping on trees, dropping to the ground.

Britain's days are happy,
But, can't say that about the night.

Keisha Johnson (13)
Chestnut Grove Visual Arts Specialist College

Britain

B usy roads although the pavement's worse,
R ich and poor both different they curse.
I nseparable dirt clings to the British floor,
T his life we live through the British door.
A bominable Prime Minister that just doesn't listen.
I n and out of entertainment with admission.
N ow that's what I call Britain!

Jordan Cummings (13)
Chestnut Grove Visual Arts Specialist College

I'm A Busker!

I'm a busker
I play my instrument
In Leicester Square
In the morning
People just watch and stare
As if to say
'Why don't you have a proper job?'
But I don't care
I play to put smiles on faces
Like the people that come
In the afternoon
They come and appreciate
They actually stop and listen
They understand the pain
The happiness
And the romance
Of my music
In the evening
That's when the children come
I love it
They dance
They sing
And make me feel good
That's why I'm a busker.

Michaela Pusey (13)
Chestnut Grove Visual Arts Specialist College

British Culture

Buses, trains,
Trams, planes.
Cats, dogs,
Gangsters, thugs.

Rubbish bins,
Littered streets.
Dirty buses,
Stuffy tubes.

Hooligans, pub-goers,
Beer-bellied men, smoking teenagers,
Screaming toddlers,
Crying babies.

Traffic jams,
Congestion charges,
Delayed trains,
Drunken brawls.

Homeless people,
Rich people,
Posh people,
Spoilt people.

This is the British culture.

Gbenro Williams (13)
Chestnut Grove Visual Arts Specialist College

The Land I Live In

Rubbish, rubbish, all around,
In the bins and on the ground,
Walls smeared with garish colours,
Spewing offensive messages about mothers.

Dogs sniffing, birds eating,
What a mess we're creating.

Cans, papers, cigarette butts discarded,
Chips and burger buns,
Pizza slices, toppings all gone,
Cans of lager, smelling evil and strong.

Homeless people behaving mad,
No one's smiling, they seem so sad.

But listen; Britain *is* a place of beauty,
Seeped in history, greatness and unity.

Fear is what makes us muddled,
Banish it away, don't be puzzled.

Look at the parks, look at the trees, look at the sky,
Feel the living cooling breeze;
Feel the love, feel the joy.

Stand in a place where history was made,
Where people believed love and fairness was all
And compassion wasn't a swear word at all.

That's the Britain I know and love,
Where education and hard work
Will make you rise above

And remember, don't look down on anyone,
Unless you're helping them up.

Lamara Forder (13)
Chestnut Grove Visual Arts Specialist College

Mysterious Music

Spiritual,
   emotional.
      Violence,
   today's music:
Pop,
   rock,
      reggae,
         R 'n' B,
            garage,
      what shall I listen to?

It
   must
      be
         mysterious
            music
               through
                  my head,
      I hear blastful beats,
      I hear mumbling melodies,
      I hear holy harmonies.

It's
   wonderful!
         It's
            beautiful!
      Where is it going?

I
   don't
      care,
         it's
            amazing.
              I
                 love
                   it!

Rebecca Boateng (14)
Chestnut Grove Visual Arts Specialist College

A Sporting Chance

Talented and most are youthful,
Those that are old but they've been there before,
Experts from the past,
There's those with quick learning,
Wonderful goals from a variety of players,
Tense and exciting but most people cry,
There's those who are coming to the future,
They might be skilful or fast but they can show class,
Too many clubs to choose from,
Some are in the Premiership, others Divisions or Conference,
England are improving their games,
It shows that they're working better together,
They're trying to show world class,
Facing countries around the globe,
People might be racists,
But players such as Campbell and Heskey try to ignore them.

Ryan James Loney (13)
Chestnut Grove Visual Arts Specialist College

Britain Today

B usy roads all around
R ubbish always on the ground
I rritating beggars asking for money
T he weather never looking sunny
A lot of different cultures roaming around
I ce-cold weather; sometimes hitting the ground
N ice people, big population, that's Britain!

Daniel Day (13)
Chestnut Grove Visual Arts Specialist College

Food For Thoughts

Indian, Chinese, Japanese and pizza,
Which one should I choose from on a Saturday night?
There are so many to choose from Indian,
Curry, chicken, rice, sauces, sweet 'n' sour,
Chinese, special fried rice, chicken chow mein.
This country isn't so plain.
I'd better get it, before I regret it.
My food's getting cold,
By the time I choose I'll be old.
Indian's nice,
Chinese, alright for the price.
There are so many to choose from
I think I'll have the lot.
When I eat all of that,
I'll probably start to drop.

Sarah Murray (13)
Chestnut Grove Visual Arts Specialist College

Notting Hill Carnival

Crowds
Music, dancing, amazement
Drinking and laughter
Everyone's having fun
Everyone's happy
Full of joy
No fights,
No killings,
All about celebrating,
For this lifetime occasion,
Let's enjoy.

Leigh Richards (13)
Chestnut Grove Visual Arts Specialist College

Fashion To The Fore

Fashion,
    Fusion,
        Black and
            White
           Versace
        Gucci
    That's
Alright

                Cash
                  Cards
                    Expenses
                     Bills
                     Stress
                  Dresses
                Shoes
              But
           No
         Heels

                         Watches
                     Rings
                  Trainers and
                Skirts
              Wear
            Everything
          Else, but
        That's
      Too
    Short

Funny
    Joy
        Clothes
           And toys
           All
              To
                Do
                  With
                    Fashion.

Toyin Douglas (14)
Chestnut Grove Visual Arts Specialist College

Notting Hill Carnival

Notting Hill Carnival means a lot to me;
Dancing, music, salt fish and ackee;
The excitement, the laughter;
Makes the crowd go wild.
The adults, the children;
That beautiful girl's smile;
The thrill;
The celebration of all these shows;
The stalls, the sound;
The streets, the clothes.
The music, the beat, the rhythm;
Setting deep inside your mind,
The drinks, the crowd, a place to socialise.

Cheriece Simpson-Tracey (13)
Chestnut Grove Visual Arts Specialist College

Food For Thought

Indian, Chinese, Japanese
All on a Saturday night
What one should I choose?

Curries are nice
Especially for the price
Come and get it
Before you regret it

Pizzas are cheap
So come and eat
Hot, cold and spicy
What do you think?

Pick one or a
3 course meal?

Leanora Josephs (13)
Chestnut Grove Visual Arts Specialist College

Notting Hill Carnival

Every year there is Notting Hill Carnival,
People from all over the world come to Notting Hill Carnival,
Different foods from all over the world,
Different stands of music, reggae, hip hop, dance etc,
Everyone dancing and having a laugh,
Getting very drunk and smashing their bottles
Which leaves lots of glass,
Remember everyone is welcome to Notting Hill Carnival.

Cheryl Rama (13)
Chestnut Grove Visual Arts Specialist College

Food, Food

Curry, spices, fish 'n' chips,
Everything is tasty too,
I love all but which one shall I choose?
Curry, spices, fish 'n' chips,
I will take . . .
All of them!

Farzana Khan (13)
Chestnut Grove Visual Arts Specialist College

Advice

Your words came back to me last night
In the heat of an argument
And I did not regret them in the cold of the morning light
'Never go to bed mad
Stay up and fight.'

Olivia Sudjic (14)
City of London School for Girls

Pastiche

(Pastiche Poem formulated from 'The Road Through The Woods', Rudyard Kipling and Autobiography, Louis MacNiece)

Before they planted the trees
My mother wore a yellow dress,
Of a summer evening late
And now you would never know.

In my childhood the trees were green
And the badgers rolled at ease
And there was plenty to be seen,
Seventy years ago.
Now the lamp is dark beside my bed.

My father used to wear his collar the wrong way round
And I'd hear the swish of her skirt on the dew, when I was five
The black dreams came . . .
The old lost road through the weeds . . . the chilly sun.
The dark was talking to the dead.

Weather and rain, they shut it down again.
Nobody, nobody was there.
You would never know.
They did not care when I awoke,
To the beat of a horse's feet and
The misty solitudes,
Saw me walk away alone,
As though I perfectly knew,
The old, lost road through the woods.
Gentleness.
It is underneath the coppice and heath

And the otter whistles to his mate,
Come back early or never come.

Eleanor Sorell (14)
City of London School for Girls

To Remember My Nights

My soul grows ablaze with the flame of a once love,
Battered and bruised it emerges,
Suffocated by elapsed memories,
My skin caressed by moonlight.

My thoughts tumble,
Arching and capering in a perplexity of dreams.
My heart blushes as I retreat from the night.

I wail,
A slip of my eyelids submerges the world
In the barren twilight of my senses.
The pinpoint too fat to recognise my state,
Amid grotesque visions and clammy repose.

As I conclude my enigmatic dreams,
Sheet entangled with feet,
I steal away from vengeful night,
To salute the infinite speckles of golden light,
Teasing the windows of my soul,
To cast back their curtains
And lose my flame now dimming,
In the settling dust of my bones.

The sun illuminates the disconcerted sky,
As my tormented eyes stifle back tears
And I remember my nights.

Jenny Atkins (15)
City of London School for Girls

A Lost Identity

I started at the spotless corridor floor,
My head bowed down to the ground.
I felt lonely and lost as always,
My ears twitching for the touch of a sound.

I walked on . . .

I stopped as I came to a window
And concentrated on a dot of light.
I wished on it with all my heart,
That same thing I wished for every night.

I walked on . . .
I stopped as I came to a clock
And longed for its assuring tick.
The thing that had never let me down, did
And I suddenly felt so sick.

I walked on . . .

I stopped as I came to a mirror,
What had happened to the person I knew?
I looked on at my clear reflection,
But my eyes watered and blurred my view.

I walked on . . .

I thought back to a time, not long ago,
When I was outside the walls of this place.
I saw stars and heard ticking, as I rested on someone,
Whilst that 'someone' tickled my face.

I walked on . . .

Juliana Tarpey (14)
City of London School for Girls

Over The Rainbow

You dragged me over the rainbow
And I did come, if rather reluctantly.
I got there and I saw that
No grass I'd ever seen before
Was as green as the green I've seen
Under your feet;
And I knew that I
Shouldn't have been reluctant
To slide over the rainbow
Because you were with me
All the way.

If I'd stayed
Behind the rainbow
I would never have
Seen shooting stars;
I would never have
Felt a snowdrop in a desert;
I would never have
Known a field filled with such flowers;
I would never have experienced
Sitting in the grass
Surrounded by flocks and flocks
Of vibrant butterflies.

And so I am glad that
I followed you over the rainbow
And I'm sorry
I was reluctant.

Flora Easton (13)
City of London School for Girls

There's One Of Two Possibilities

There's one of two possibilities:
Either you do it or you don't.
If you do that's okay, but if you don't then
There's one of two possibilities:
Either you get found out or you don't.
If you don't then that's okay, but if you get found out then
There's one of two possibilities:
Either you run or you don't.
If you run then that's okay, but if you don't
There's one of two possibilities:
Either you get caught or you don't.
If you don't then that's okay, but if you get caught then
There's one of two possibilities:
Either you go to prison or you die.
If you go to prison then you might escape, but if you die then you
Will never know.

Lottie Thompson (14)
City of London School for Girls

Watch The World Go By

Put your head against your pillow,
Allow your heart to grow and billow,
Let no one weep except the willow.

Put your mind in a trance,
Watch the fairies turn and dance,
Your head can play and leap and prance.

Ignore all sayings, sit and stare,
Become an empty room, blank and bare,
Stroll around without a care.

Think of clouds in the sky,
A misty moon, a firefly,
Why imagine? Why not try?
Sit and watch the world go by.

Mikaela Green (12)
City of London School for Girls

Reflection

Looking in the mirror,
I can see
My reflection,
Just the same as me
And I wonder if they'd know
Which was which
And who was who,
If me and my reflection
Stood side by side,
Or she was out here
And I was inside
The mirror
Or if she was a person
Who walked and talked -
And not just a shadow,
Which flickered and stalked
- On this side of the glass
Could anyone see
That she is my reflection
And I am
Me?

Emma Knowles (13)
City of London School for Girls

Black

A dark haze,
Separated, disruptive,
Another existence,
Another perspective.
Blind to the world,
Yet seeing more than anyone.
An echoing whisper,
A silence, so loud.

Uncovered,
Vulnerable,
Exposed.
Appears to be empty,
Yet full of everything in the world and more.
Unexpected,
Unfamiliar,
Unknown.
A sheet of darkness,
Containing its own light -
Only hidden.

Charlotte Salkind (12)
City of London School for Girls

The Point

I hear people talking about the point all day long,
The point of this sentence, the point of this song.
My friends say it too - 'That's not the point!' they cry.
Can someone tell me what is? Ask I.
The point could be the sharp end of a needle, or scissors that cut,
That slide into skin, make the red blood well up.
But that's not the point of this poem, this verse.
My inability to make the point has been a lifelong curse,
Teachers talk, organise points into paragraphs,
There's a point to essays, homework and graphs,
There's a point to this poem (I'll come to it soon,
I'm searching under seas, stars and moon,
For the words that communicate the point, turn it into a line
Of this poem, which I think, is somehow fine
Without a point, but there has to be, you see,
There's apparently a point to everything, to you and me.
But I'm getting off the point - which I never was on
And this poem is getting quite boringly long.)
The point of this poem, a vague little thing,
Is that if there's a point to everything,
Well, what the hell is it?

Zoe Sharp (13)
City of London School for Girls

Tiny Angel

Sitting above me, to watch how I sleep,
Do you know the pain I hold from giving you away?
I would have kept you for the entire world,
I saw a life for you.
I wanted to push you in the buggy
And swing you on the swings,
But now I'll never know, I'll never see you grow.
Sixteen is just too young,
No father is no good,
My parents couldn't handle another child,
Living in our home
I didn't have a house,
I wasn't fully grown,
But tiny angel, please stay with me
And grow in my heart
And play with my children,
So we will never part,
I feel in my loneliness you are my one friend
And even in the darkest times you're watching over me,
My tiny angel child.

Rebecca Schofield (12)
City of London School for Girls

Monlife

Television blaring its square message,
Eyes drinking in every mindless detail,
Embroidered sofa, the seat of no state,
Time passes, but in the Home nothing changes,
Stale air lies like a lazy mist on the moor,
Dust blankets all in its stifling embrace,
While I, I sit and stare, stare and sit,
Endless monotony, the thoughtless territory,
Waiting in vain for some stop, some Change.

Computer glaring, errored obscenity,
Boredom settles and mind wanders to lust,
Hand slips under mass-produced pine table,
Time passes, but in the Office nothing changes,
Eyes search, suspicion written all around,
Great sigh of content. Glance back to same screen,
Great sigh of depression, fidget phase starts,
Stationery drawn up, war of the pens,
Waiting in vain for some stop, some Change.

Whiteboard shining, reflected fluorescence,
Unfathomable, infallible data sets,
Head propped up by palm, eyes simmer downward,
Time passes, but in the School nothing changes,
The endless drone drowns any sentient thought,
Rumbles of impatience whilst time ticks by,
Slipping through my vulnerable fingers,
Each moment precious, each moment gone, yet still,
Waiting in vain for some stop, some Change.

Samuel Landau (15)
City of London School for Girls

The Beach

The silky-smooth sand flowing over my feet,
The wind like a whetted knife stabbing my face,
The lapping waves bringing forth to the damp shore,
Waves ascend from the watery monster,
Deserted, isolated, abandoned beach covered in cold damp mist,
Rising sun like a fluorescent fiery creature,
The cliffs trapping me in a sandy bay,
Jagged and sinister to all intruders,
They rule the beach with the waves and the dunes,
Cruel clouds came covering up the sun,
Pounding thunder echoing off the cliffs,
The rain making the sand spotted and patterned,
Waves surfing ferociously, touching the sky,
Then the sensation was over, maybe,
Just maybe this feeling will return one day,
When I have had my time and memories reappear.

Rachael Coomber (12)
City of London School for Girls

Talking About The Future

There's a boy from my old school,
My teacher brought him into class
And he settled down,
My teacher said, 'Let's have a trip,'
I was his partner.
We were talking about our future,
When he was talking it was like a poem,
That's why I felt I loved him,
I wished he was my little brother.

Rosabella Wellesley-Cole (12)
College Park Special School

Houda

Houda is kind
Houda is pretty
Houda is friendly
Houda is good
Houda is taller
Houda is great
Houda is nice
Houda is lovely
Houda is helpful
Houda is always speaking to me
Houda likes playing with me
Houda likes speaking to me
Houda likes going home with me
Houda likes doing work with me
Houda likes doing work by herself.

Yasmin Nessa (12)
College Park Special School

Poem Of Myself

I am Ayesha
I am adorable
I am a girl
I like macaroni cheese
I like rice and curry
My age is 13 years old
My favourite subject is English, art and ICT

I like Sue, she is my English teacher
She is my best teacher for the whole year
Jenny is an associate teacher

I like reading, spellings
And computers.

Ayesha Sultana (12)
College Park Special School

Alone On An Island

I am cold
I need food
I need to drink

I feel very lonely
From my rucksack
I pull my sleeping bag

It is dark blue and warm
I fall asleep quickly
I hear the sounds
Of the waves on the beach

The wind is howling through the trees
I think of home
I think of my family

I think of my friends
I think about my school.

John Couroussopoulos (14)
College Park Special School

The Game

Football is a game
For people to play
And enjoy teamwork
Players are winners or losers
But they all play their best
It doesn't matter if you are
A good or bad player
Just as long as you try your best.

Christopher De Freitas (11)
College Park Special School

Enjoy School!

I like bunking off
But
I like playing football with my friends
I enjoy doing maths work
I enjoy doing PE and art
I am funny sometimes

I like going anywhere
But school
I like basketball
I like joking with my friends
I enjoy doing ICT
I like English

I like running away from the cops
But
I like doing DT
I enjoy doing RE
I like working on computers
I like helping teachers sometimes

Now I write more than 14 lines.

Hussain Ali (15)
College Park Special School

My Poem

The grass is green, the sky is blue
I like Harry Potter, why don't you?

Harry Potter is the best, so are girls,
Why don't you like Harry Potter too?

Jackelene Hartigan (11)
College Park Special School

Me At School

Me in Year 10 *talkative*
To people

Me in Year 10 *loud*
In lessons

Me in Year 10 *helpful*
To my friends

Me in Year 10 *funny*
Making my friends laugh

Me in Year 10 *kind*
And generous

Me in Year 10 *caring*
For my friends

Me in Year 10 *thoughtful*
And trustful

Me in Year 10

Working hard.

Wasima Elhabti (14)
College Park Special School

Football

I like to play football every day
As I have school I cannot play
I play on Saturday and Sunday too
Maybe one day I will play for Man U!

Elyes Chalf (11)
College Park Special School

Me At School

Progressive
Stressed
Tired
Rude
Angry
Sleepy
Talkative
Brainy
Loud
Bored
Funny
Disruptive
Worried
Competitive
Delighted
Active
But I enjoy every minute.

James Hogan (14)
College Park Special School

The Football Match

My name is Sidiki and I like football,
I like passing the ball to my team mates,
After we score the goal.
Me and my friends made a plan,
About scoring and passing to each other
Until we score,
Then we play the football match.
After we play against other people,
Who want to play against us.
I hope we win and be happy,
Me and my friends went home
And we told our mums and dads,
We had the best day ever.

Sidiki Sanou (11)
College Park Special School

Untitled

Alone, on my own and I'm feeling scared,
Leaning on a part of my boat hull,
Only me on the island,
Now setting up camp,
Eating the leftover of my crew members' lunch.

Only half a day past and it feels like Hell,
Not much chance for survival, I'm slowly dying.

I'm wasting away, all I know is that
This island has no water,
Sadly my best crew member died, I cried.
Last ounce of strength in my body,
I scream as loud as I can
And then this man wearing black shorts
And a black T-shirt,
'Not possible,' I said.
The man said, 'You're on my island!'
Days went by until a rescue plane
Came and I was rescued and brought home.

James Watson (13)
College Park Special School

I Like

I like playing football.
I like doing art.
I like maths.
I like to go on holiday.
I like to have fun.
I like to go on school trips.
I like to run about.

Dean Gaudin (11)
College Park Special School

Me At School

In Year 7 I was smart and good
When I'm angry I go mad and bad
But when I'm in class some people go mad
But some people were nice

In Year 8 my class got put on report book
If we were bad we stayed inside
If we were good we got to go outside and play
If we were good for the whole week our teacher took us out to the café

In Year 9 my class was good
We were off the report book
Some people did work and were not silly
My work was getting good
I felt happy when I did more maths work
It is my favourite subject

Now in Year 10 I get worried when I do a test
My work is getting harder, harder, harder and harder
I get confused when I do the questions
Some questions are easy
And some questions are hard
But I hope to pass my test.

Roben Quiambao
College Park Special School

A Piece Of The Pie

Just a world full of lies
and someone dying
for that piece of the pie

He's down, he's hurt
so he tries to stay alive
and keep his eyes
on the prize.

Billy Kelly (12)
College Park Special School

For My Mum

I like my mum because she cooks nice food,
She cooks *great* chips.

She takes me shopping and to the park,
She buys me a nice jacket,
In the park I play with my new ball.

When she is cooking food, we *talk together*,
We talk about school and my packed lunch.

I am *very happy* because she gives me nice clothes.

Micky Solomon (15)
College Park Special School

Kings Of Africa

L is for the loud roar it makes when hunting
I is for its instinct used to catch its prey
O is for the order it demands in the pride
N is for the way it nurtures its young

   Put them together they spell *lion*
   One of the great kings of *Africa.*

Phillip Higgins (11)
College Park Special School

The World Today

Why am I here
In a world with fear?
Could it be that our
Leaders still don't care?
So I would pray
For you my dear
For better times
I swear.

Choukri Ellekhlifi (12)
College Park Special School

Getting The Blame For No Reason

One day my cousin came to my house
Also that day we had a party in Southall restaurant
I was looking forward to it, but I could not go because I had
To look after my little cousin
So my mum and dad didn't want to leave me on my own,
But I told them to go and I said to Mum and Dad
That I can manage,
Also I made a big mistake, I said I could manage,
My cousin told me to let him on my PC
But I said no, he got upset,
He said it was alright, then I went to the living room
Watching TV, he went to my room
Deleting all my things from my PC,
My cousin's things as well,
Everyone came from the party,
They saw the PC was blasted,
I got the blame, that broke my heart
And no one trusted me anymore,
But I took my revenge on my cousin,
I deleted his things as well
And I blamed him, he was grounded,
He was not allowed anywhere except school,
My mum and dad also my cousin's brother
Found out it was not my fault,
He broke it, I was happy that my family knew
That I would never do something like that.

Shitar Miah (16)
College Park Special School

Family

I love my mum
Because she is fun
When we're in the sea
She splashes me
She makes me laugh
When we're walking down the path
Because she makes funny faces at me

My dad's name's Paul
He is cool
He is a builder
He likes playing pool

I have two sisters
They're down to earth and cool
They help me with my homework
Whenever I need it or anything else at all
I'm excited, my sister is having a baby

I had a nan
Now she is in a better land
She passed away to a better place
And with no pain
I miss her so much
I wish she was here
But that's just hoping
My wish will not come true

That is my family
As you can see
I love them
As much as they love me.

Emma Potter (15)
College Park Special School

About Me In Year 9 And 10

In Year 9 I'm friendly to people,
In Year 9 I am funny when I make people laugh,
In Year 9 I'm feeling shy
Sometimes when the people ask me something,
In Year 9 I take it seriously when people call me 'Fish-lips' sometimes

Now in Year 10, I sometimes get nervous when
I do a lot of coursework,
It started changing my life to do something new.

In Year 10 I am still talkative,
In Year 10 I'm starting to work hard
And to become more clever.

In Year 10 I grow up more nicely
And become more beautiful.

Marti Buenaventura (14)
College Park Special School

Alone

Alone on an island
I don't know where I am
Nothing to wear, nothing to eat
Nothing to drink
I am so tired, I need to sleep

I am alone
I don't know what to do
I am so sad
Where am I?

I wish my family were here
I wish my friends were here
But I'm all alone
Just me.

Ella Parker (13)
College Park Special School

I Am On An Island

I am feeling happy and sad
I picked some fruits from the jungle
From the forest I find fresh water
I feel lonely, I miss my friends
I make a bed out of leaves
I fall asleep and dream of home
When I wake up I am on the island.

Natalie Bleau (13)
College Park Special School

Alone On An Island

I see a rose-red fairy
She smells nice
Starlight perfume
I am hungry
She helps me
She brings me tuna sandwiches
And strawberry cakes.

Waleed Marmar (13)
College Park Special School

The Story Of Love

It is strange to think
I haven't seen you for a month
I have seen the new moon
But not you
I have seen the sunset and sunrise
But nothing of your beautiful face.

Kamel Cherkowai (13)
College Park Special School

A Strange, Empty, Lonely Island

Alone on an island with nothing left in my pockets,
Sad, cold, hungry and tired,
I search, search but all I find is wood and stones,
I cry, cry, help, help.

Rescue me, take me to a restaurant,
I'm starving man, I would have a fine time,
But that's daydreaming,
That's not going to happen.

I look up at the stars at night,
Maybe find out what's on the island,
I never know what I might find,
But I will keep on wishing day by day.

Meera Main (13)
College Park Special School

The Colour Of Rainbows

On the island there is yellow sand nearby
By the sea there is not lots of shore everywhere
Lots of shore and me

There are lots of birds on the island
Trees, I can see mangoes
Hanging yellow like they're ripe

The pineapples are beautiful yellow
Like the colour of the sun

Everywhere brilliant colour
In the trees, birds, green, yellow, red,
Trees the colour of rainbows.

Reba Begum (13)
College Park Special School

Feeling

I am feeling hot
I am looking for food
I am angry
No one to talk to
Lost all my friends
I feel like crying

Missing my family
Thinking of them all day
Wishing, wishing, I was at home
I shall go to bed now
But worrying how I will
Escape from this island

I wish my mum could come
Then all the family would be
Happy.

Rosemary Kelly (14)
College Park Special School

When I'm At School

When I'm at school I make my friends laugh,
When someone needs help I'm sympathetic.

When I'm upset I am really serious,
When someone tells me off I get angry.

I am miserable when I think about something bad,
I am happy when I'm glad.

My friend Marti makes me laugh then I'm happy,
Because she's a good mate I feel calm.

Rehana Bibi (14)
College Park Special School

My Sister

My sister is like my best friend
She is always willing to lend a hand
Best friends are my sister and me
We laugh, we cry
We never lie

We share all our things
Our laughs, our secrets, our problems
And our thoughts
I am so thankful to my sister
For her loyalty, her love and her warmth
Thinking of her brings warm
Feelings in my head and smiles
In my day

Times will change
And so will we, but our bond will never break
I will always be thinking of you
My sister
My friend
You are my inspiration
My friend for always
Having you as my sister
Has been very important
My whole life through

I would like you to know
I appreciate everything you do for me
I will always be there for you
I will always be thinking of you
I love you
Always.

Sabeen Hussain (12)
Connaught School for Girls

My Mummy

When I was a tiny pea,
My mummy introduced me to the world,
She was sweet as an apple pie,
Which crumbled
In her mouth,
I couldn't see or even hear,
But I know that my mummy will be with me when I need her.

As years went by I grew bigger and bigger,
I was nearly tall as a giraffe with a tail,
Which itched a lot,
But my mummy would always make it better,
By licking my tail with a toffee-flavoured tongue,
Golden syrup would come dripping onto my tail,
It would always come with a big splash.

I was now wiser and stronger,
But my mummy was going weaker and older,
Her soft fur was not as soft as it used to be,
Instead it was like human's skin,
I could see the wrinkles around her eyes,
It was time for me to look after her,
Her legs were stiff as wooden poles,
She couldn't move or even hear,
But she knew that I was with her.

She was now weak as a dead plant,
It was her time to rest in peace,
She closed her delicate eyes,
There was silence as a pin drop,
But then there was a tear in my eye,
It dropped from my face onto her,
But I knew that my mummy would watch down on me from Heaven.

Aneesa Mehmood (13)
Connaught School for Girls

Tragedy!

It took a long time for my life to heal,
with all the secrets and lies that were revealed.
When summer slipped away it became worse,
because my dad was so ill, he needed a nurse.
My mum had lied,
the secrets were bad
and as each day came
I felt sorry for my dad.
We hardly had any money, my mum didn't care,
all she wanted was her share.
It suddenly snowed,
I couldn't go out,
we needed milk and bread
and Brussels sprouts.
The nurse had bad news,
but I was confused,
my dad became so ill,
there was nothing she could do.
The snow didn't stop,
the wind became vile
and every phone number we tried
it would not dial.
My dad only had one sister,
she lived in New York,
but because of the phone,
they couldn't talk.
The worst thing was,
my mum had lied
and after a few weeks,
my dad had died.

Amina Siddique (12)
Connaught School for Girls

Friendship

(Dedicated to Emma, Emily and Jade)

Some people call us the blondies,
We prefer awesome foursome!

Some would call us mad,
Others would call us crazy!

What I know is
We're great friends!

Of course we have our ups
And our downs!

We have our fights
And also the make ups!

They call us a group of friends
But they are wrong,

We are a friendship,
A real friendship!

Clarice Hilton (12)
Connaught School for Girls

The Clear Blue Sea

The sea is clear, as clear as can be
There are lots of different creatures we can see
Dangerous creatures far and near
Everyone screaming, people hear
The sea is blue, as blue as can be
People love it, just like me
There are lots of different coloured creatures all around
Some of them are waiting to be found
Seaweed is green, the sea is blue
I love the sea and hopefully you do too.

Mirella Nammour (11)
Convent of Jesus & Mary Language College

The Beach

The beach is so nice,
I wouldn't mind going there twice,
When I know I'm going to the beach,
To the stars I want to reach,
The gleaming sun,
That to the water makes you wanna run
Is so wanted at home,
When you're drinking water on your own.

When you wanna go somewhere,
You know it's always there,
Tempting you,
To make your dream come true.
Sometimes it's tough because
People just can't have enough.
If you're sad at the end of the day,
Just think that next time is just one day away.

Emanuela Gomes (11)
Convent of Jesus & Mary Language College

Nothing Compares!

I have been in love before,
But nothing compares to this,
You've touched my heart,
In places that others always miss.

As long as time keeps on passing by,
My love for you will never end,
You will always have a place in my *heart!*

Vanessa Adjei (11)
Convent of Jesus & Mary Language College

Sweet Shop

When you go into a sweet shop,
Shelves are full of jars,
In those jars are strawberry laces,
Lemon sherbets, fizzy cola bottles
And lots, lots more! (Cor!)

The sweet shop is like a palace,
A palace full of sweets,
I want to live in a palace of sweets,
Sweets for breakfast, sweets for lunch
And sweets for dinner,
Even my bed is made out of sweets,
But that's only a dream.
Good (burp) night!

Franchesca Manaloberdin (11)
Convent of Jesus & Mary Language College

All Around The World

All different foods
All different places
All around the world
All sizes
All shapes
All around the world
All skin colours
All personalities
All around the world
We are all different
But all the same
We are *one!*
All around the world.

Molly McInerney (11)
Convent of Jesus & Mary Language College

To The Heavens Above

Grandfather from above
Look at me now
The world seems so different from down here!
From the hours I've cried
To the hours I've smiled
You'll always be there in my heart
From the moments of terror
To the moments of joy
You'll be there
That little laugh you used to do
That's what the angels will like about you
But whatever happens
You're still in my heart
The last time I saw you
You were in bed and you said
'Sorry I can't come'
But you knew I would always love you
Plus I'll see you again next year
If these words were true
You would be here with me now
But from this date 26 September 2001
You left me here alone
And went to the heavens above!
A part of me has gone
And I didn't say goodbye
But now some years have passed
And I'll never say goodbye
For now you're here forever
And forever you'll stay in my heart.

Yasmin Benourida (11)
Convent of Jesus & Mary Language College

Clap Those Hands To The Beat

Clap those hands to the beat
And stamp those fancy feet
You should scream out loud
And make the biggest crowd
Clap those hands to the beat
And stamp those fancy feet
Eat your veg all the time
That means you are doing a crime
Clap those hands to the beat
And stamp those fancy feet
Always play football
And you know that you will go tall
Clap those hands to the beat
And stamp those fancy feet
If you are kind
You can drink wine
Clap those hands to the beat
And stamp those fancy feet
If you like rum
You should just come
Clap your hands to the beat
And stamp those fancy feet
Listen to the cans
Doing their loud rhymes
Clap those hands to the beat
And stamp those fancy feet
It is time to go to sleep
And make your sleep very deep
Clap your hands to the beat
And stamp those fancy feet.

Anaise Collins (11)
Convent of Jesus & Mary Language College

A Poem Of Love

I love you
And I know you love me too
I look above
And I know you are giving me love
I give you a kiss
On you sweet lips

I will give you some tea
If you say you love me
And you can have my house key
I know we can be together
And it will last forever
So why wait?
It's like a piece of cake

So now we have made our love
So now I do not have to look above
We shall be together forever
And ever
And ever

You are my number one
So don't try to run
Because I love you.

Rebecca Dover (11)
Convent of Jesus & Mary Language College

Ocean

I was walking along the ocean shore
The sun shining in my face
The waves crashing at the rocks
Isn't the ocean a wonderful place?
Children laughing and playing
Parents chatting, love based
Happily with their mates
Isn't the ocean a beautiful place?

Sammy-Joe Meredith (12)
Convent of Jesus & Mary Language College

The Sea

I stand on the beach staring at the sea
Wondering what animals live in the sea
From morning to night, I sit on the beach
Wondering what sort of creatures would be standing
And waiting for me

Under the sea, I wanted to be
But as far as I can see I could not be
Whenever I see a creature that pops up
To be seen whenever I get close
It's never to be seen
Silent as I can be, I wait to see any creatures
From the sea, I think to myself
What would it be like being a creature of the sea?

When I see the sun go down behind the sea
I'd like to be one of the creatures
To see the sun go down behind the sea
I wouldn't mind being a sea creature
Because it sounds awfully exciting.

Karen Udeh (11)
Convent of Jesus & Mary Language College

School

School is hard
Work all day
Finishing school late
If you're late 15 minutes
Twice a week is 1 hour
Some teachers are nice
Some are horrible
Can sometimes be very tiring
And I want to go to bed.

Henna Talbutt (11)
Convent of Jesus & Mary Language College

Dogs

Dogs, dogs, dogs,
they run about after balls,
twigs, sticks and cats.

Dogs, dogs, dogs,
they come in all shapes and sizes,
fat, small and plump.

Dogs, dogs, dogs,
their fur can be soft,
matted, mangled or smooth.

Dogs, dogs, dogs,
their bark can be high,
middle, quiet or low.

Dogs, dogs, dogs.

Sinéad Dwane-McCann (13)
Convent of Jesus & Mary Language College

Just Me

I am myself and myself is who I am
No one is like me
I am unique, if I had a magic box
I'd put a tooth from a dolphin inside
Five special wishes
The bright yellow sun
And a shell from the golden sand
I like lilies and bluebells
Red roses too
Running and swimming
How about you?

Shanice Adams (11)
Convent of Jesus & Mary Language College

A Sunset

The sun is setting in the sky
The moon is coming to say goodnight
The sky is purple, orange, red and yellow
It is a magical sunset
Nothing so wonderful as a sunset
The colours are so vibrant
The colours remind me of a huge 76
Exploding in the sky

Go to sleep, when you wake it will be
A huge ball of fire
Coming to brighten your day.

Katie Moore (11)
Convent of Jesus & Mary Language College

My Cat

My cat is white and black
Always bringing home mice
Never ever had lice
Playing with a ball of string
That is the really strange thing
Unwinds it for miles
All over the tiles
He loves his food
Always in a good mood
He is very soft
Always chasing moths
That's my cat!

Athena Hall (11)
Convent of Jesus & Mary Language College

Hallowe'en Is Here!

Hallowe'en is here!
Time to prepare!
Black cats and witches' hats
And maybe even spooky bats!
As wolves howl and bark
And as colourful fireworks spark,
Trick or treat or defeat!
The end has come to Hallowe'en,
So goodnight and don't let the bedbugs bite!

Tara O'Connor (11)
Convent of Jesus & Mary Language College

The Ocean

The ocean is blue, blue as the sky,
You can watch it all day form morning till night,
Sea creatures crawl in the oceans,
Enjoy their life, be happy as they can be,
Oceans are filled with many creatures
That live in the ocean,
Watching out for others.

Raquel Ribeiro (11)
Convent of Jesus & Mary Language College

Two Little Sisters

Two little sisters went walking one day,
Partly for exercise, partly to play,
They took with them kites which they wanted to fly,
One a big centipede, one a great butterfly.
Then up in a moment, the kites floated high,
Like dragons that seemed to be touching the sky.

Sarah-Jane Cyrus (11)
Convent of Jesus & Mary Language College

Before One

On the day of my birth,
My father swore an angel,
Carried me into the room
And placed me in his arms,
He was so happy,
The thought of changing my nappy
Did not phase him at all,
I was so small I fitted into his hands,
No problem at all,
Little did he know I would grow tall,
My father swore I was a miracle
He gazed at me and gazed
Not realising I was growing by the minute.
I started to smile,
I made my first sound,
Grew two teeth by the time
I was three months,
Then I started to crawl,
Once again my father was happy,
Amazed all at once,
He praised me again,
He even learnt how to babble
And chuckle in the same way as me,
When I was 10 months,
I started to walk,
My father told everyone once again
He was happy
And still changing my nappy
Did not phase him.
I was now smiling,
Babbling, chuckling and walking too,
I could say, 'Mum, Dad' and 'ta-ta',
Then on my next birthday
I became one.

Rianne Camille (11)
Convent of Jesus & Mary Language College

Night And Day

Gently as the moon goes by,
The stars call out to sigh,
The angels blow their golden horn,
Come sun, come out for it is dawn.
Happy as the sun may be,
The stars and moon they disagree,
But as the sun comes to an end,
The stars and moon will shine again.

Stephanie Jarvis-Ampoto (11)
Convent of Jesus & Mary Language College

Love

Love is a mystery,
No one ever worked out,
Every time I see you,
Hear your name,
When you look at me.

There is no guilt between us,
No such thing at all,
You and me here at a romantic,
Fascinating French dinner.

I am over-excited about you as you are for me,
This is my first time,
I must be humiliated and embarrassed,
Don't laugh at me.

Me and you spending so much time together,
Boat riding, swimming, arranging dinner,
Sending real tulips and staring into other's eyes.

I am over the moon about you,
I hope we stay in each other's arms
Forever and ever . . .

Bushra Begum (12)
George Mitchell School

War

War, why do we adore it so?
As young men stand row in row

Up on the front line
Their hearts are pumping
I feel it as if it was mine

Bang, bang! goes a gun
The war has begun
And now they want to turn and run

Doctors, nurses are on hand
Ready to help those on land

The rain comes down *thud, thud, thud*
As men in green run through the mud

The war has ended
We have won
Soldiers cry, 'Yes, yes
We are done.'

Katie Davis (12)
George Mitchell School

Orange October

Orange October
Branches walking in the wind
Leaves lying around
Early darkness gets closer
Like a ghost creeping in the night
Smoke drifting in the breeze
The wind takes us away
The cold weather forces through me
Tiredness
It gets darker much earlier
Orange October
A time to surrender.

Mandeep Kalsi (13)
George Mitchell School

Two Faces

When I look back into the past,
I see horses being whipped and horses being stroked,
I think, *why this?*
What will I grow up to be?
I lie back in my bed and quicksand pulls me in deeper and deeper.
Then I turn to see dark trees surrounding me,
I turn to hear pain, anger and misery,
I don't know what to do!
The noise is killing me,
I can't take it anymore, I jump to my cold feet.
I scream so loud, I can't get my senses to the atmosphere,
Then my eyes snap open,
I see things, objects,
The skies are bright highlighted blue,
I can see shapes in the clouds,
I drop on my back.
Have I forgotten my senses one second ago?
No, that's impossible.
I scamper to my feet and run towards the awful noise.
I see animals, creatures I have never seen before,
The air has love floating in it,
I see caring for one another,
Then I see some sort of light swimming across my eyes,
I shudder for a moment and never want this feeling to end,
I slowly open my eyes but close them rapidly,
But I don't feel the love around me.

Syeda Hussain (13)
George Mitchell School

Another London Day!

Another London day,
All the clouds are dark and grey,
No patch of blue sky,
No birds flying high,
Men in black ties
And miserable sighs,
Oh another day in London.

The hustle and bustle of London streets,
The busy sound of many feet.
Umbrellas go up as cold rain comes down,
Wet shoes trudge through puddles as they scrape on the ground,
Oh another day in London.

The dark blue ocean and crashing waves,
The sunlight glistening on window panes.
White fluffy clouds float way up high,
As streamlined birds soar through the sky.

Mountains of dreams,
Fields of gold,
People together,
Young and old,
United as one, relaxed in the sun.

Why can't London be like this?
Why can't London be like home?

Luba Salpetrier (13)
George Mitchell School

Figure Thirteen

Suffocating, stifling
Hands grasping for the razor
Cold against scarred skin
The first breath through pain . . .

Grasping, searching
Tears streaming down isolated face
Feeling for invisible shoulder
No contact, no warmth . . .

Numb, cold
Frozen inside out
Through artery, through vein
Through mind, insane . . .

Bare. Exposed
Wind grabbing skin
Cliff the gulf
Between life and death
Peace and pain . . .

Falling. Broken
Ocean spray like needles
Biting into bone
Soul leaving mind
Eternity gone, time left behind.

Husniye Has (15)
Hackney Free & Parochial Secondary School

Rap Is Life

To make a well-liked poem you need the main ingredients,
Metaphors and similes, imagery, alliteration and personification,
Are the key ingredients for a delicious poem.
It keeps the words flowing
And the rhymes pumping.
So your beat never stops.
Remember rhyme is rap
And rap is life.
So if you like rap, don't forget to rhyme.
Poetry comes from the heart,
It comes from deep within the soul.
Just like a love song, it needs passion,
Affection and most of all honesty.
It won't stop as long as you keep believing.
So get a pen and some paper ready,
To write a waterfall of flowing words.
Remember rhyme is rap
And rap is life.

Tanesha Bryan (12)
Hackney Free & Parochial Secondary School

The Old Apothecary

Coldly, he hovers over the deadly fumes,
Making the sweet taste of death.
He wears a black mask to stop himself from breathing in
The stench of the deadly drink.

He slaves over the poison,
Day and night not knowing
When to stop because of the overwhelming
Feeling of the gold coins in his crooked hand

Each day a person comes seeking revenge
On their hated enemies
When a young, attractive woman walks in
The old apothecary's eyes shine with excitement
And suddenly a lopsided smile appears on his face.

Carlesha Whyte (15)
Hackney Free & Parochial Secondary School

Colours Of Beauty

Autumn has come around,
Like the Earth moving on its axis fluently rotating.
The colourful leaves that have an intense composition,
Sparkle in the fascinating sunlight,
Spreading colours of reds, gold, green and yellow.
It is as though an elegant rainbow
Has painted a picture of a paradise scenery,
Leaving an impressive and inspirational, vivid poem of Heaven.

Then winter will crash in and everything will die,
With vulnerability and coldness, turning the ground hard and frosty,
Fulfilling hopes and dreams.
The air will freeze as if it is imprisoned in ice and wind,
Leaving shivers and misty breaths travelling through the open space.

Abruptly spring will displace it
And glamorous flowers will blossom and bloom
And the sweet scent, flowing like a naked river,
Will make your stomach rumble with hunger.
The chirping of the amiable birds
And the buzzing of the tranquil bees
Will set all nature's problems free, the river's bank will burst
And a baby blue glistening and glorious appearance,
Will quench all thirsts.

Summer then kicks spring out of the way
And the scorching sun will kill the rain and the clouds
And the sky will deliver an imperturbable message,
To those who understand it.
The trees will rustle and sway to the rhythm of the world,
Like an audience would if they were in concert.
This is the colour of beauty, surrounding me and my environment,
Enclosing my life and my future.

La'neshia Dubois (13)
Hackney Free & Parochial Secondary School

What Type Of World Are We Living In?

What type of world are we living in?
A world of hate and so much sin.
People fighting and people killing,
Don't you see, it's the wrong song we're singing.

All around the world there are wars,
Ask yourself what is it all for?
Our world leaders are fighting,
Why can't they do the right thing?

It must be crowded up in Heaven,
Remember September eleven?
All those people that died, didn't survive,
Left loved ones here on Earth to mourn and cry.

September eleven shocked a whole nation,
Think what the world's going to be like for the future generation.
The terrorist that did this, one question, *why?*
We could all live in peace, we just have to try.

There are people in the world with nothing to eat,
They don't even have anything to wear on their feet.

It's unbelievable, they have so many needs,
Look at us, we do everything in greed.
All these things that are going on,
Can't you see there's something seriously wrong?

Things need to change, we need to put things straight,
Things need to be changed now, before it's too late,
What happened to caring and loving one another?
Don't you see we're all sisters and brothers.

Things need to change real quick,
It shouldn't be like this, it makes me sick.
Just stop and think about all these things,
Then ask yourself, what type of world are we living in?

Evangelene Jegede (15)
Hackney Free & Parochial Secondary School

Try

The mountains were as gigantic as the solar system,
My feet were stamping like elephants about to be fed,
I thought I'd never make it up the mashed potato-like mountain,
But then I thought, *why give up for I'm as strong as these mountains,*
They'll never beat me because I'm determined to make it.

My purpose is clear as ice-cold water,
I'll find them if it's the last thing I ever do,
They're mysterious as magic
And as interesting as a circus of sofas!

Koral-Leigh Webb (11)
Highams Park School

The Playground

Children running up and down,
Little ones on the grounds.
Looking for the footballs,
Teachers giving frowns.

Chatting to each other,
Eating and gossiping.
Their voices getting louder,
Till the teacher starts shouting.

Then the bell rings for lesson five
And everyone goes dashing in.
Hoping not to be late,
As that would be a sin.

Hannah Carter (12)
Highams Park School

The Witching Hour

Cats staring,
Eyes glaring,
Owls scowling,
Dogs howling,
In the light of the full moon.

Shadows sneaking,
Floorboards creaking,
Silhouettes talking,
The dead walking?
At 12.00 midnight.

Adults grunting,
Foxes hunting,
Children dreaming,
Demons scheming?
In the house near the old graveyard.

Bats flapping,
Spiders tapping,
People turning,
Vampires yearning?
On October 31st.

Cats staring,
Eyes glaring,
Owls scowling,
Dogs howling,
In the light of the rising sun.

Poppy Clark (12)
Highams Park School

I Remember . . .

I remember
My first footsteps
A holiday to Spain
No regrets
An old home
A cradled baby
All alone
A special teacher
Operation
A horrid creature
Party
A sleepover
Black belt in karate
Wedding bells ringing
Big brown eyes
Relatives singing
Crying
Red room
A friend lying
A nice sweet
A hug
Trick or treat?
A gold star
A charity
A nice chocolate bar
Polished medal
Business card
A breaking pedal
A shiny new bike
Rainbow
Trainers from Nike
A mobile phone
A funny moment
A sarcastic tone
My favourite video

Shopping
A broken toe
An art project
A shoulder to lean on
A funny object
Help from a family member
These are the things I shall
Always . . . remember.

Emily Dillon (14)
Holy Family Technology College

I Remember

My first bike,
A holiday away,
A very long hike,
Friends to stay,
A day at the Dome,
A day at the park,
A night at home.

I remember . . .
My baby steps,
Playing in the depths,
Playing in the snow,
Going so low.

I remember . . .
A day in the sun,
Playing with friends,
A night with Mum,
A rainy day in.

I remember . . .
The good days away,
I remember holidays,
I remember going to play,
I remember.

James Dietz (14)
Holy Family Technology College

I Remember . . . I Remember . . .

I remember when I went on holiday
My family and I needed to get away
It had a swimming pool
And a table to play pool
The hotel was quite big and tall
I thought the place was really cool

I stayed there for about a week
Me and some friends played hide-and-seek
At night I went into the town
The street acts reminded me of clowns
The buildings were a shade of golden-brown
As I walked I looked around

I woke and saw a lovely sun
This is great, I'm having fun
Right at the pool the kids would run
I had a swim, a nice cool dip
And with my drink I took a sip
I fell down, I had a slip

I wasn't having fun anymore
My head was split and ripped and torn
They pulled me on the red-soaked lawn
I went into the hospital
I told them that I'd had a fall
My head was pounding I felt small

I had eight stitches in my head
At that time I thought I was dead
All I could see was red
I wasn't allowed to swim anymore
My head was really, really sore
I really wanted to swim more

My holiday was ruined
Next time I'll be careful
And remember not to run
Even if I'm having fun
I should just stay safe with my mum
Especially as I am still young.

Jason Norris (14)
Holy Family Technology College

I Remember . . .

I remember . . .
The day we first started talking
I had known her for quite some time
Properly we started talking
Over some little game or something
Acting like friends but now we were

I remember . . .
I met some other people then
Well, they lived next door to my friend
Two boys who I got on well with
They became my friends that same day
This was how I got to know them

I remember . . .
Now it's almost been a year since then
That happened on the six-week break
I have always loved that time of year
There is no school and lots of fun
It's just so great, I love it

I remember . . .
My holidays, sun, sea and fun
I had great fun there with my mate
A nice morning walk on the beach
We went out and looked for crabs
I see him on my holidays

I don't remember . . .
How I stopped talking to people
I like having friends to talk to
I like hanging around with them
But what I don't understand is
How I lost some friends that I knew.

Ryan Adams (14)
Holy Family Technology College

Do I Remember?

I remember when I was six
I was on the see-saw
When . . . when I fell onto the metal bar
And I cracked my tooth
And when I got up, my mother was full of blood
It hurt so much that I had to go to the hospital straight away
I remember how much it hurt
And all the pain that just shot through me
I felt like I had a big lump in my mouth
This is something that I can always remember
Although not to remember it as a good thing
This is too much of a bad thing
But I will still remember

How can I write about what I don't remember?
If I could remember then, then I could write about it
But I don't remember
Maybe if I keep writing then maybe I could remember
I think . . . I think I remember
Or, or maybe I'm just imagining that
I can't remember what I was going to write . . .
Why does this have to be so, so complicated?
I don't know why this is so hard
It's only a poem - I guess
This is nothing like a poem
Nothing rhymes, well, does it have to?
I don't know
Maybe I should ask someone what to write?
Or maybe not
They might not be able to write anything either
But if I don't know what to write
How am I supposed to finish this poem?
Maybe I should finish this poem here
But it needs to be longer
Maybe . . . maybe not

I don't know
If I carry on writing then I won't know what to write
Although this may be long enough
Because if I keep writing, I will be writing too much
I don't know what to do
Hmm . . . you know what?
I'm going to stop here
That's if I can remember my poem.

Tracy Andrews (14)
Holy Family Technology College

I Remember

I remember when my mum was not well,
I remember when I had a big party,
I remember when my dad left my mum
And I remember when I fell and broke my thumb.

I remember when I was in hospital,
I remember when I got a needle.
I remember when I bought my rabbit
And I remember when I had a bad habit
But least of all I am me.

I remember when I had my communion,
I remember when I wore a beautiful dress,
I remember when I fell out with my mate
And I remember when I went to a huge fete.

I remember when I turned thirty in August,
I remember when I liked this boy at school,
I remember when I had my confirmation
And I remember when I got a certificate at a presentation,
But finally I remember being *me*.

Bernadette Vahey
Holy Family Technology College

I Remember

I remember when I went to hospital to have my first operation,
I remember all the nurses and doctors that helped me get better,
I remember all the food and all the flowers I had sent to me,
I remember my mum and dad sleeping on an old bed
And then getting up after no sleep and going to work,
I remember all the laughs and the happiness.

But I also remember all the pain and suffering,
All the drugs and medication and all the treatment I went through,
I also remember the suffering my mum went through
To watch me in agony.

I remember the car journey home and the trip up the stairs
That took five minutes but felt like five hours,
I remember all my friends coming to visit me and making me laugh,
I also remember them sneaking me sweets even though
I wasn't supposed to have any.

I remember my first steps,
I remember my first words and phrases,
Even my first day at school,
I remember phone numbers and addresses
And all the important birthdays.

But what I remember most, I want to forget
And what I forget I want to remember most,
So, what do I do?
Well -
I *don't* remember.

Lewis Mamooya (14)
Holy Family Technology College

Growing Up

I remember when life was fun
you could spend all day just playing in the sun

I remember life without a care
when you weren't happy to share
when you wanted everything to yourself
she's yours, nobody else

I remember first days at school
I remember not wanting to leave
I'd made friends
what's at home for me?

I remember growing up
I remember my first crush
I remember feeling blue
when it seems no one's there to comfort you

I remember the arguments day after day
The judges' vote I just couldn't sway
I remember not caring at all
I remember hearing the beckoning call

Now I remember it as all in the past
What was I thinking!
I'm glad the feeling didn't last.

Kayleigh White (14)
Holy Family Technology College

I Remember

I remember the days when I used to be your friend
I remember the days when I used to play pool

I remember the days when we were together
I remember the days when I used to see you

I remember the days when we used to ride our bikes in the park
I remember the days when we would walk in the park

I cherish the days when I was with you
I cherish the days when I was in your company

Now you're in a better place
And no longer living in this world

Years have gone by since your death, I've made new friends
I still always think about you a lot
But I've moved on
But I still feel lonely and unhappy
But I still have memories.

Louis Blackwood (14)
Holy Family Technology College

I Remember My Family Splitting Up

I remember each row, every fight and every cry
I remember exactly how I kissed you goodbye
I remember each stop as you walked away
I remember you only each night and day
I remember the pain, the hurt and the sorrow
Not wanting to see another tomorrow
I remember it all, to the endless tears
All the worries, the bitterness, all of my fears
But I remember no doubts, nor any regrets
And I remember the promise that I would not forget
That I would hold you and keep you so close in my heart
And remember why you chose for you to part
Though you will always be part of me
I will always remember that I set you free.

Charlie Reed (14)
Holy Family Technology College

I Remember

I remember the day the fun we had as we danced the night away
I remember that music blasting and everybody screaming hurrah
I remember the dares we played 19, 20, 21, 'Oh my God, it's me!'
I remember the secrets we told, even Emily became a bit bold
I remember the sweet white wine we drank all night
Unlike others it didn't cause us to fight
I remember the walk we had, grabbed a pizza and that was that
I remember the mess we made all over the carpet, still
there to this day
I remember standing by the pond, Kayleigh tossing her
glistening blonde hair
I remember standing in the street waving goodbye to everyone
But most of all I remember that thing she said about that boy
I remember the hurt, sorrow and tears
But most of all I remember the joy.

Louisa James (14)
Holy Family Technology College

I Remember

I remember when the trees were swaying, the children playing
Running around, falling down, picking themselves back up
off the ground
Cars speeding, drivers' heavy breathing
Police never caring, losing their job, never fearing
I remember when it was all about going to church
every Sunday, praying
I remember when it was all fun playing out in the rain or sun
I remember when it used to be hot, no fear of getting shot
I remember when I first broke an arm, it was at the local farm
But now I can remember about all the fun I had, I was about one
Always out on the street with mum, I had gold and silver by the ton.

Wayde Bruce (14)
Holy Family Technology College

I Remember

I remember when I was a little boy
Thought nature's wildlife was so wonderful
It makes you think, why trees fall
What could be the consequence to me?
If I were to say, go in one of the animal's cages
Would they possibly tear me up into different parts?

Who knows, they would probably do it in stages
I can vividly remember, when I was around 10 years old
A bag of sweets dropped out of my bag along the old isle road
I was embarrassed walking down the old isle road
Can anything get any better than walking down the old isle road?

I don't know, I was fond of wildlife when I was a little boy
I would have rather played when my old and rusty little toys
Would it be of any use to me if I had animal toys?
Maybe I would of screamed and shouted like a little big boy
The extravagant world of wildlife is so unpredictable
You don't know if a lion or kangaroo
Is going to leap or bite at you
You will have to wait until that situation happens to you
Hope you enjoyed this poem and hope wildlife is very fond of you.

Marlon Warner (14)
Holy Family Technology College

My First School

I remember attending my first school,
It was dreary but I enjoyed it,
Our teacher, Mrs Clark was very courteous and sharing,
She taught us how to share with each other
And how to apologise.

I remember when everyone had to hold hands to play this game,
I stood next to this girl who everyone thought stank,
I felt sorry for her because her mother was single
And they didn't have much.

I remember holding her perspiring hand,
I let go of it and wiped my hands on my little flowered dress,
I remembered the look on Mrs Clark's face,
She was enraged but what did I care!
I was only 3 years old.

I remember going home and confiding in my mum,
Boy, was she furious!
She told me I shouldn't have done that
And that I would have to apologise the very next day,
That's precisely what I did because my mum came along
                                        to see me at it,
Now 11 years on, we are still best friends.

Justine Gustave (14)
Holy Family Technology College

I Remember Walking Down The Street

I remember when walking down the street,
I remember a ten pound note at my feet.

I remember when walking down the street,
I remember seeing someone cheat,
I remember that time in November
Or come to think of it, was it September?
When it started to snow,
People said, 'What a great show!'
That time when I was walking down the street.

When I walk down a street,
Sometimes there's people I'd like to meet,
Young and old,
White or black,
Even the old man who carries his sack.

When I walk down the very long street,
I see different people start to eat,
I see lots of people starting to greet,
Down different types of roads and streets.

Kevin Bergin (14)
Holy Family Technology College

I Remember

I remember your face
I remember your smile
I remember your laugh
I remember your voice

I remember when you shouted at me
I remember when you kissed me
I remember when you hugged me
I remember when you called me

I remember your last few weeks
I remember your last few days
I remember your last few hours
I remember your last few minutes

I remember when you went
I remember the look on your face
I remember your last words
I remember you said, 'I love you'

I remember that I said
'I love you too, Mum.'

Dane Crook (14)
Holy Family Technology College

Wanting To Forget

I remember you, with your perfect smile and perfect taste,
What you said to me the first time we met,
And how everything just fell into place.
I know what you want, and why you want it,
I can hear your voice still echoing around my head.
And I remember life beginning with flowers when you walked in
I remember you, with the diamonds in your grin
And how all the world began to spin.
But I don't remember wanting you near me,
I don't remember wanting to see you,
I can't feel what you say you do
Parked in your small Mini, watching me walk away
I don't remember asking you to like me, or hate me
I don't remember asking you to exist, I can't escape your entrance
And the smell of roses still there, and I can't escape the diamonds
That spill from your mouth
I remember how life began, but I don't remember you . . .

Chi-San Howard (15)
Holy Family Technology College

I'm So Lonely

I 'm so lonely,
M y heart desires a home.

S o would someone rescue me?
O h, how I long for a home;

L onger than my imagination;
O h, please someone find me.
N o longer can I stay here in this filthy box,
E ver waiting for a place in a heart,
L onger and longer I wait,
Y earning for a home.

Spencer Jevon (12)
Joseph Clarke School

Swimming With The Dolphins

Swimming with the dolphins,
Being pulled along by its fin,
Swimming to the lagoon side,
I'm sure you will like him.

Swimming with the dolphins,
Watching them do a flip,
Swimming back beside me
And resting by my hip.

The dolphin's name was Tyler,
He was a happy chap,
Every time he performed a trick,
He expected us to clap.

Swimming with the dolphins,
It's something I have done,
It was unforgettable
And Tyler's my special one.

It's an experience I will remember,
Until the end of time,
I still dream of you often,
Tyler, oh how I wish you were mine.

Thomas McMillan (11)
Joseph Clarke School

If I Were A . . .

If I were a piece of furniture,
I would be a feathered gold armchair,
In the Queen's palace,
Keeping her warm and comfortable,
While listening to her personal orchestra,
Playing in the grounds of her palace.

Faye Linay (11)
Joseph Clarke School

Shark Attack

I was swimming with the sharks,
I got a nose bleed,
A doctor, a nurse, a specialist I need.
My leg's in his mouth now,
It feels kind of funny,
He's bitten my shin,
He's rubbing his tummy.
I'm really quite flabby,
The equivalent of chips,
If he were like me,
He'd have fat hips!
He's shaking his head,
Like in disapproval,
He's had enough of me
And ready for removal.
So next time
You're swimming with sharks,
Remember . . .
Don't get a nose bleed!

Jazz Branford-Dennis (11)
Joseph Clarke School

If I Were A . . .

If I were a piece of furniture,
I would be a warm bed,
In my nan's house,
I would be keeping her warm,
When she needed it most,
Feeling happiness to know that she was there and she was fine,
While listening to her sleeping peacefully.

Jason Morris (11)
Joseph Clarke School

Dave The Brave

There was a pilot called Dave,
Who found it hard to be brave,
One night in the air,
While eating a pear,
He swallowed a pip,
Which gave him jip
And all of a quiver,
He started to shiver,
He had to land
In really bad weather,
They said that the plane,
Came down like a feather,
Now he's 'Dave the Brave'.

Scott Barthram (12)
Joseph Clarke School

Football Crazy

Football crazy, football mad,
I really like it, so does my dad,
People call it out of date,
But I think football is really great,
Eleven players on a pitch,
Each one of them is very rich.

Kieran McGarry (11)
Joseph Clarke School

Cats

Furry, cuddly, warm and friendly,
Black and tabby, white and ginger,
Stroke them, play with them
Or hold them on your lap,
Cats are great, we love them too.

Nyle Okebu-Stewart (11)
Joseph Clarke School

I Want To Be A Singer

After leaving school I want to be a singer
I've always wanted to be a singer ever since I was a beginner
To have my name in lights
All through the night
And listen to people sing the songs I write
Yes, singing is my dream but it has not always been
I wanted to be a designer and design clothes for the famous
But I don't think I could deal with all the drama and lateness
I wanted to be a chef and cook to my best
But I don't think I could beat or be better than any of the rest
So now I know that wherever I turn
I will always learn
That these jobs are not for me
No matter how much I earn

I want to be a singer
To show you what I can be
I want to be a singer
Only singing can satisfy me.

Jhozette Samuel (14)
Kingsmead School

Home Is . . .

Home is . . .
Home is where I am at peace,
Home is where I am with my family,
Home is where I keep my secrets,
Home is . . .

Home is . . .
Home is the place I cannot live without,
Home is my retreat from the world,
Home is anywhere I get these feelings,
Home is . . .

David Gathard (15)
Kingsmead School

I Love Home

I love being at 'home'
It's the best place to be
There is lots of support and comfort
With the most warmth I need
We have lots of fun times
And also some sad
We have lots of happy times
And rarely any bad
Home is where I get help
And given lots of love
Home is where I'm cared for
It is so much fun.

Cassie Robinson (14)
Kingsmead School

Home

A place of reality, where no one lies,
A place where there's comfort when someone cries.
Somewhere you're happy and free,
Where you can be who you want to be.

A place where what's yours is mine,
A place where you can twinkle and shine.
Somewhere there's love and care,
Where things aren't always that fair.

Home is where you feel safe and secure,
Home is the certainty when you're unsure.

Alex Bailey (14)
Kingsmead School

Love Is . . .

Love is the air in Finsbury Park
Love is watching the sky spark
Love is being near to someone you love in the dark
Love is . . .

Love is the flower that blooms in spring
Love is the bluebirds and robins as they begin to sing
Love is everything that gives you a warm feeling
Love is . . .

Love is sitting and watching time fly by
Love is having something catch your eye
Love is then being able to give a relieved sigh
Love is . . .

Love is the feeling that you gave to me
Love is the thing you stole from me
Love is finally being able to truly see
Love is . . .

Love is a she, a he, an it
Love is even the person you called 'git'
Love can even be throwing a fit, but is that what
Love is?

Moses Fapohunda (14)
Kingsmead School

By A Moment

We were so complete
We met at a party
It was love at first sight
The body language said

We were so complete
The love was deep as an ocean
Shone like a star
Nothing could tear us apart

We were so complete
Every moment we spent together
Changed everything for good
My days were cold without him

We were so complete
His kisses made my lips quiver
His touch made my whole body shiver
He drove me insane

We were so complete
I couldn't believe what was happening
Is this true?
I asked myself over and over again

We were so complete
How could he do this to me?
Break my heart into a thousand pieces
My first love, true and real love

We were so complete
He had been cheating on me all this time
What a fool I had been

We were so complete
On the cliff edge, I thought of jumping
I held myself back
I now know life could be changed
By a moment.

Diana Mutanho (14)
Kingsmead School

The Face Outside My Window

Every night I see her
Her icy wild stare
Her hands against the window
I know why she's there

Her hair like shining water
Her eyes so stoned and black
The insane smile she smiles
I try not to look back

I turn away from the window
To block out the ghostly being
I do not want to fall asleep
It's her that I keep seeing

I know that she's after me
As she scratches the windowpane
Her hunger to claw at my flesh
Her complexion so madly insane

I try to sing myself to sleep
But she sings a chorus back
She tries to meddle with my mind
Willing to attack

My heart begins to panic
My pulse beating one by one
She's not at the window anymore
I don't know where she's gone

I hear a chorus in my ear
And a heavy knock on my door
My heart skips like a snake on fire
And this is what I saw

The transparent figure stood there that eve
Her lips curled enviously
My body begins to tremble
She's coming, she's coming for me . . .

Nicola Tozzi (13)
La Sainte Union Convent School

Friends Of The Future

You can talk about Atlantis
or what's lost beneath the sea,

The grave of the unknown soldier
or the cry of the old banshee.

Who was the man in the iron mask?
and was Jack the Ripper set free?

But ask them all about peace on Earth
and it's still a mystery.

What about war and these horrible weapons,
who knows what's really where?

What really matters in life
and who really cares?

To hear that we walk free,
would give me such a thrill,

Or that world peace and love
was over the next hill.

So don't despair because if you dare,
the answer lies with me,

We can each make a difference,
if we let our minds be free.

We must love one another
and live for the here and now.

Warn about each other
and peace will be found somehow.

Forget about what's happened
and all the troubles past,

Let's put it all behind us
and make new friendships that will last.

Paula O'Dwyer (12)
La Sainte Union Convent School

Babies

Babies! Babies! Babies!
All they ever do is
Cry! Cry! Cry!
Drool! Drool! Drool!
Eat! Eat! Eat!
Cry, drool, eat!
Drool, eat, cry!
Eat, cry, drool!
Attention?
Seek, seek!
You should be lucky to even grab
A good night's sleep
With one of them around!
Oh babies!
Baabbiieess!

Natasha Otto (11)
La Sainte Union Convent School

The Waterfall

It flows hard
As fast as a dart
It tips over to the side
And at the bottom it collides
Then it goes back to calm
Like a little baby calf
I think I might of guessed what it is
But a few more clues I shall give
It will be kind and calm
Then normal and lovely
Have you guessed what it is yet?
Of course! It's a waterfall!
That flows and flows and flows.

Sandra Atimokidi (11)
La Sainte Union Convent School

Changing Seasons

Blossoms bloom and colours appear,
New found flowers are shooting here,
The sky is full of chirping birds,
Spring has come with the new herds.

The sun is blazing, the sky is blue,
A different season has sprung anew,
Summer has come and it comes fast,
People enjoy the heat at last.

Seasons come and seasons go,
Swirling leaves move to and fro,
Mountain peaks and turquoise seas,
High and towering autumn trees.

Snowflakes, glistening droplets from above,
Speckles of snow fall down like doves,
Sheets of snow upon the floor,
Winter will last for evermore.

Denise Osei-Kuffour (12)
La Sainte Union Convent School

I Miss You!

I miss you every day
Every second and in every way
When I think, I think of you
And all the things you used to do
I look at your picture and think a good thought
And remember the times when we have fought
I'm saying sorry for the things I have done
And say to myself and ask, 'Why was I so dumb?'
When you moved and turned away
I couldn't see the light of day
I'm so sorry in every way
So can you come home straight away?

Brooklyn Quinn (13)
La Sainte Union Convent School

Innocence

Born softly good like baby.
Embrace young angel with sacred kiss
And dance as translucent champagne oceans do.

Question peace and speak like haunted child,
Make a window to the universe
But only explore blushing stars above.

Devour yesterday.

Squirm at perfumed wake.

Remember,
Worry less,
Be blind, yet not to deep decay.

Celebrate fresh smiles
And learn.

Roisin O'Reilly (17)
La Sainte Union Convent School

The Wood

There I lay on the cold dark grass
Suddenly I awake
I look around not knowing where I am
Then I realise I am in a wood
I get up feeling scared
Not knowing what to do
Then I find myself running
Trees surround me
I run on and on
Trying to escape
But it never ends
Their branches reach deep inside my soul
Taking me into their depths
I scream but I can't be heard
I dread that I have become the wood's spirit.

Ilda Abi-Khalil (12)
La Sainte Union Convent School

My Love Is Real!

The pain I feel is painful
When my love is not there
When will I see him? When and where?
How will I go to find my love?
When will I see the bright white dove?
Will I seem to see him first
Or will I seem to see him last?
When will I see him? I've got to see him fast,
When I first saw him, it was love at first sight,
Though it was morning, I felt the distance of the night,
When will I see him?
I have got to see him now,
I can't wait any longer,
But where, when and how?
I have dreams of my love holding me tight,
The footsteps appear as I see my black knight,
I love him more than life itself,
I want to be with him and it's not because of wealth,
I have a dream he loves me a lot
And we marry, I can't explain how I feel,
Just for now and evermore, let's hope this dream is real.

Rebecca Oduah (12)
La Sainte Union Convent School

Spring

A drop of rain is now enough
The colours of the flowers now have opened
Sky birds poke out their heads in delight
Of the sun's light

Out comes the sun
In delight to see the amazing colours
Of the spring's flowers.

Sabrina Babo (11)
La Sainte Union Convent School

The Night Is Long

His eyes so pretty,
He sings a lovely sound,
His hair is spiked
And his nose ring is round.

Outside he stands,
Just waiting for me,
Playing a guitar,
Just under the tree.

I hear him playing,
In my aid,
Singing a song,
Under the shade.

I walk out the door,
Holding a light,
He kisses my lips
And says goodnight.

Alison Fernandes (12)
La Sainte Union Convent School

You Know Who You Are

You're prejudiced and you discriminate,
You've gone too far and it's too late.
Clearly we are too unlike,
I like skateboards, you like mikes.
You hold it against me,
But one day you will see,
I am right and you are wrong,
Though it might take you long.
To whom this is addressed,
I hope that you are blessed,
This is to stop you making the same mistakes twice,
I don't dislike you, I just want to help you.

Katherine Wise (12)
La Sainte Union Convent School

Battle Of The Somme

Young men marching
Like lambs to the knife,
With guns fully loaded
To obliterate life.

Make it past that,
To die soon after,
Silencing their cries,
Silencing their laughter.

Women at home,
Not accepting to learn,
That there is no hope
Of their loved one's return.

Your chance of living
Are one million to zero,
But if you keep going,
You'll die like a hero.

Why is there hatred?
Why is there war?
Why can't there be peace
For now and evermore?

Katy Tobin (12)
La Sainte Union Convent School

Through The Window

Through the window I can see,
Young people, old people,
Rich people, poor people,
Kids throwing things at the pizza van,
Wash me graffitied on a van
Blue car, red car,
Gold and silver.

Through the window I can see,
Cigarette butts on the ground,
Glass bottles dropped make a crashing sound.
Forgotten couches and washing machines,
Patches of grass,
Brown not green,
Motorbike, tricycle,
Moped and plain bicycle.

Through the window I can see,
A park for walking and playing footie.
Dark old benches, soiled and sooty,
But at night when it's cold and dark,
There are druggies and drunks,
It's a terrible park.
Friendly faces smiling at me,
Friends I know,
Walking slowly past my flat,
That is what I see through my window.

Jackie Atta-Hayford (11)
La Sainte Union Convent School

The Great Shining Moon

Moving along looking at me,
Knowing that I can see,
He shines down with lots of desire,
Like the sun shining fire.

The moonlit trees are glittering,
As we hear the bright stars sing,
The night is really very dark,
As it has such a spark.

Grey mist passes slowly so,
Giving it a great big glow,
Its colour is so very clear,
That everyone might just fear.

So as I watch it with its light,
Shining very big and bright,
In the distance far away,
He would never speak or say.

He follows me everywhere I go,
Never thinking high or low,
Look at his pale, shiny face,
Not speeding up just takes his pace.

In the morning I look to the sky,
All the way very high,
But I see the sun,
Where's the moon?

Rachel Fernandez (12)
La Sainte Union Convent School

Freedom

The sea is spraying on my cold face,
If the world was in this place, I'd be happy.

I may be tough and hard and harsh,
I need to be loved and needed like everyone else.

All the world does is blame and scream at me,
It's hard to block it out, so I yell and shout

As loud as I can and when I stop, my eyes
Choked with tears, the silence deafens me so I

Laugh and smile happily, it can't reach
My haunted eyes which are red on the inside,

When I am alone, there's no one there to put a
Mask on for, it's just me, all alone with no one.

The mask comes off, I am revealed, finally my
Head comes up bravely, vulnerable but calm.

Sea that roars before me, all fight I don't have,
Water in my mouth, salt in my eyes, a blindness

I don't, I cannot resist, who would resist freedom?
I sink to the bottom and become still and at one

With the earth, my brain gives a final attempt
Then shuts down, a blankness occurs, peace at last.

Hayley Teixeira-Roxburgh (13)
La Sainte Union Convent School

The Poet

In a little dark room a poet would sit and write,
Write throughout the unspoken hours, till no longer daylight.
He'd sit and wonder dumblessly till he'd write what sounded best,
Feeling useless and unclever he slumped on his desk.

But that was when it came to him, the words of great sound,
'Wait for me! My only hope, I shall come to thee!'
The wind whispered into his ear ever so silently,
He wrote non-stop using his blunt quill,
Everything was extremely quiet and the wind was ever so still.

The sky was ever so dark, only to see the night light moon
And still the poet was writing, in his little dark room,
He wrote until his hand was tired and could not write anymore;
He carried on writing until he could not take anymore.

In a small and little dark room a poet would sit and write,
Write through the unspoken hours, until it was daylight.
When he finally finished his poem, he didn't think about rest,
He got up and stretched himself then went back to work on his desk!

Vanessa Gawaran (12)
La Sainte Union Convent School

Haven From Harm

So this is the refuge to which we fly,
Seems more comfortable than meets the eye.
Greeted by squalor and penury,
Blamed for violence and robbery.
We seek a new life away from harm,
But all we get is the voice of alarm.
Our names are swiftly and subtly dismissed,
In a media coloured with prejudice.
Mirth and myths plague us day and night,
Distorting our past and our pride.
Jobless and insecure are we,
We only want a place of warmth; a family.

I Mieng Wong (18)
Leyton Sixth Form College

Emerald Eyes

Beautiful and gleaming
Hateful and streaming
    With tears
The truth, a smokeless flame stroking tainted ears
The stained glass screen
A façade hiding deepest fears
And muffled screams
Beneath a blanket of porous dreams
    Which perish
And turn to dust at first light of dawn
Which on that morn
Bore witness to the bitterness born
    The day
The Earth and Sky, which once were one
Siamese twins joined at the soul - were finally torn
And left with so much more
    Including a gaping hole
As though something was missing
    One thing, which would make them whole
And so each yearned to have what the other possessed
Empty desires which when fulfilled are left cold with no meaning
The Earth draped in a beautiful cloak of green
Awoke to find it flooded with the dew of a thousand years
Wiped away by an invisible hand from the eyes of a colourless sky
Which failed to hide
The dismay of having nourished and bought to life
The one thing she had lived for and sought to destroy
For absent now is the warmth and heart of the sun
Present only is the moon - a reflective reminder
                of self-destructive vanity
And the stars, twinkling emeralds seeking insatiable beauty.

Mbalu Saine (17)
Leyton Sixth Form College

The Foreigner

I'm the foreigner, the abused foreigner.
I felt like eating, but there was no food.
I only eat burnt crumbs of rice, if at all I'm considered, and
In return I do excessive housework.
No education, no friends, no life.
Only constant abuse.

My family fractured by divorce,
My life turned upside down.
At six, I was alone.

Still alone, at fifteen,
I fly high above the clouds to
England and freedom

But new stepparents did not mean a new life.
At seventeen, I live a life
Dominated by a bully.

Beaten for calling my stepfather
'Sir', I live a life of confusion.
A foreigner, an abused foreigner.

I walk the streets, fear stalking my footsteps.
I hear voices screaming 'Deportation.'

Black eyes in white faces
Stare back at me, uncaring.
How long must I be an abused foreigner?

Abdul Karim Jabbie (17)
Leyton Sixth Form College

It Could Be Anything But Mean Everything

A big valentine's card with unfinished
writing, written in a bright red pen

which was found broken in two.
It was in two pieces just like

when your heart is broken,
that thing was a heart-shaped cushion.

The picture had a person missing,
maybe because the other person did

not return, in time, the same feeling.
In a tall red vase was one

very pretty and fully blossomed rose
but the colour was hard to tell

because it was really dry and old.
The message may have been short

but it was just as beautiful
as the diamond eternity ring.

The message ended with the words
'You are my all and everything.'

Bilkis Begum (16)
Leyton Sixth Form College

Always On My Mind

Happiness fills my soul
Laughter I can't control

. . . Always on my mind

Talking with no cares
Walking with no fears

. . . Always in my heart

Refreshingly so sweet
Each time we meet

. . . Always in my thoughts

Protection from all bad
Shoulder when I'm sad

. . . Always on my side

Subject of my dreams
Silly, though it seems

. . . Always on my mind.

Falon Paris (18)
Leyton Sixth Form College

The One And Only

Are you the one for me?
To satisfy my needs
And fulfil all my fantasies
Allowing me to live out all my dreams.
To be there in times of trouble
And appreciate me,
Even when I'm mean.
To love and to hold me
Through the good and bad times
To tell me it's okay
When I'm worrying out of my mind.
Will I give you the chance
To prove this to me?
Only the not so distant future will see.
Are you destined and meant to be
The one and only person for me?

Lorraine Watson (17)
Leyton Sixth Form College

My Feelings

The rattle of the mighty chains,
The roaring of the angry rain.
The screaming of the many dead,
The silent laughter which is said.
The masks, the faces,
From far and many places.
The people with so many surprises,
Keep us alive, alive.
The quietness which is asleep,
Midnight's hour comes to peep.
People in all different disguises
It's a mystery and our story flies . . .

Sheun Oshinbolu (11)
Little Ilford School

Racial Division

As I approached the traffic lights
My heart pounds as I pray I
Won't get into a fight.

Stray boys come to clean my windscreen
To give it an awesome sheen
But the lights go green
And off I go so relieved
Down the road easily deceived of what I can see
Red flowers draw nearer to my nose
As I pull my window to a close
And luckily for me the green light shows
As I get to well-paid place
I see aside these rugged clothes
And as I draw closer I turn my face
In total and utter disgrace.

Why are we separated by our race?

Your race
My race.

Pardeep Singh Lall (14)
Little Ilford School

True Love!

I sit at night and think of you
Wonder if the feeling I have is true?
When I sleep, I hear your name,
When I wake, it starts again.
Hearing your voice is like seeing light
But then it's dark when you're out of sight
Cannot live if it's not with you
And the way I feel is certainly true
But the question is, do you love me to?

Anish Mandalia (14)
Little Ilford School

I'm Not Scared Of Life At All

Hearts of the chain shall not feel pain
And all their love shall stay above.
Like when you come next to me, it's like a bliss,
I tried to catch you and I missed.
I wet my path with tears like dew,
Weeping for you when no one knew.
I crossed your path and I lost control,
But then you held on to my soul.
And know I'm not scared of life at all,
Noises down the hall,
Shadows on the wall,
I am not scared of life at all.
Evil dogs barking loud,
Devilish ghosts in the clouds.
I'm not scared of life at all.
You're the one I love, and will always desire.
Somehow, all the pain you put me through,
I would slowly take in and admire,
A hand I can hold,
With a smile so dear,
A heart's that so true,
I have nothing to fear.

Asma Bhol (15)
Little Ilford School

Friendship

Friendship is a scave through yeas of
Joy, laughter, happiness and tears.
It's a work of art - priceless,
It's shared by a precious few,
Yet easily created by a loving friend like you.

Rohima Uddin (11)
Little Ilford School

Children In Need

What would you say if you saw
A child on the street,

Begging night and day, nowhere to sleep?

These are the children that people neglect
I think these children need respect.

These children need a house so please
Pick up the phone.

What would you say if a child came up to you?
Would you say go away or would you say please stay?
A small girl of ten living in a den with one brother and no mother.

Please don't turn these children away
They might not live to see another day.

Nabeeha Khan (11)
Little Ilford School

I Am The Summer

I am the summer
that switches on the light.

I am the summer
that turns on the heating.

I am the summer
that welcomes her friends.

I am the summer
that helps her friends grow.

I am the summer
that encourages children to come and play.

I am the summer
that goes to the beach.

Rumana Begum (11)
Little Ilford School

Frankenspine

Once upon a time,
In a town on the Equator Line,
Lived a kid by the name of Frankenspine.
Now Frankenspine was a bit of a boff,
There wasn't a thing he couldn't pull off.
So Frank said it was his intention,
To amaze the world with a great invention.
So he couldn't decide just what it should be,
So he bruised his brain saying, 'Let me see.'
How about a human that leaves no trace,
Or what about a mask to change your face.
Perhaps a clock that always shows quarter-past nine,
Or a pair of boots to help you climb.
What about a flying saucer made from bits of rocks,
A crazy contraption for making socks,
'Nah,' said Frank, 'that's no fun,
That's all adult stuff, that's all been done.'

How can you call him bit of a boff,
If there were things he can pull off
Because he has a spine, his eyes do blink,
Soon after it will help to think,
So here it goes!

Once upon a time, in the town on the Equator Line,
Lived a kid by the name of Frankenspine!
Now Frankenspine wasn't a bit of buff,
There were lots of things he could pull off!
So Frank has no invention,
To destroy the world with his worst intention!
So I am warning you or else he'll be with you!

Mahvesh Rana Javaid (13)
Little Ilford School

I Pray!

There's this special person deep down in my heart,
Every day and night he's in my mind,
No matter how many girls he has,
I still love him,
In my heart he's always mine.

Even in my sleep and every dream, he's there,
As days go by, the pain just increases,
There are no words that can describe the way I feel -

How much I love him . . .
How much I miss him . . .
How much I want to be with him . . .

But there is no way I could tell him,
Because he's out there in a lonely world.
No one to talk to, no one to hold.
I wish I had a way to tell him,
The way I feel,
But I don't think there will ever be a time.

I can feel a rage of fire,
Burning in my heart,
I wish he could come this moment and light it out
And make all my dreams come true.
I can't get him out of my head
And when I am with him,
I feel like I can touch the sky!

Every night I pray,
I pray to Allah to see the person one day.
One day that I could tell the person,
How much he means to me
And that I cannot live without him -
For even one more day.
Delicate!

Jahanara Begum (12)
Little Ilford School

Cinderella

Poor Cinderella sat inside
Her sisters thought of her as the opposite of kind
She scrubbed and scrubbed
Working so hard
Locked in the house
Feeling as dead as a mouse
Hoping her sisters would change their ways
She carried on cleaning for many days.

One day a letter came in the post
Inviting her to a place she loved the most
They did not want Cinderella to show
The three sisters wanted to marry the prince
Although each one looked as ugly as 'The Grinch'

Cinderella cried on her kitchen floor
She could not believe it when she saw
Her beautiful godmother
It could be no other
Cinderella done as she was told
Her clothes no longer looked like mould
She knew she had to be back by twelve
Unless she wanted the prince to see wrong
She got into her golden coach and hurried along.

When she got to the ball
She heard the prince call
It was love at first sight.
After they danced
It was time to go home
The prince started to moan
Her glass slipper dropped onto the floor
Avoiding this she ran some more
The next day the prince went round
When he got to Cinderella she was proud
The glass slipper fitted perfectly
Cinderella married the prince happily!

Priya Kanabar (14)
Little Ilford School

The Mystical Box

(Based on 'Magic Box' by Kit Wright)

I will place in my box . . .
The crystal teardrops of a unicorn,
The fire from a dragon's mouth,
The soft music on a sunset.

I will place in my box . . .
The cry of a blue whale,
The song of a lost mermaid,
The sound of a harp.

I will place in my box . . .
The laughter of my friends,
The cries of my foes
And screams of the people who
Deserve to be punished.

In my box are things that
Can never be in any other,
It's kept safe,
Deep in my heart . . .

Sehar Nizami (11)
Little Ilford School

A Friend Who Cares

When I think of all the things
You have done for me

And many times you listened and cared.

I realise just how lucky I have been
To have a friend like you.

Thank you for being such a good
And wonderful friend to me.

Rukshana Ali (12)
Little Ilford School

Mirror Image

I take a look in the mirror
But what do I see?
I stare and stare
All that is there is a reflection of me
The colour of my skin can be read like a book
Am I black, white or Asian based on a single look?
My Bengali culture is all around me
But to others I'm just a fishy odour
Which shouldn't be set free
My beautiful sarees and shalwar kameez
Are left to stand at the back of the wardrobe
All because people laugh and tease
How I wish this pain would ease
I look at the mirror and a tear of sadness
Runs down my 'curry face'
It takes so long for people to realise
We're all part of the human race
They don't accept us for who we are
And I don't understand why
I look out of the window in search of the answers
I see a rainbow form up in the sky
And realise that the world is full of so much colour
If we were all the same . . .
The world would be so much duller!

Shuhena Bhanu (13)
Little Ilford School

Dolphins

Dolphins are the cutest
Probably the nicest
I know many other species
But dolphins are the best!

Dolphins are lovely of all things I know
They're ever so harmless,
Unlike the others,
Species of all others are likely to bite!

Dolphins are the cutest
Surely the best
With all its tricks it'll beat the rest!

Shahina Khan (13)
Little Ilford School

Where I Wanna Be!

Paradise is my goal,
It is where I wanna go,
Flying high and feeling free,
It's exactly where I wanna be.

Over the rainbow is where I'll go,
Knowing what I need to know,
Higher and higher over the sea,
Going to where I wanna be.

In my eyes Heaven beams,
It's what I need to fulfil my dreams,
In ten years time that's me,
Being where I wanna be.

Jasmine Chowdhuary (11)
Little Ilford School

As Beautiful As An Angel

As beautiful as an angel
As sweet as she sings,
She flies to the heavens,
Her heavenly wings.

I know she's watching
As I lie peacefully in my sleep,
She watches as I dream
And breathe long and deep.

I can see her in my dream
She's . . . beautiful and glowing,
She sits at a table . . .
Sewing.

A long, lovely dress
Purely white,
It's lined with laces
Nice and bright.

My hand protecting my face
For the light blinded me,
The angel saw and asked,
'Can you see?'

Jodianne Taylor (17)
Newham Sixth Form College

A Poem About Water

Eternal that I am,
Giver of life that I am,
Thirst quencher that I am,
Calming the fire that I am,
Bodies' many (tears) that I am,
Forever flowing that I am,
Forever mixing that I am,
Colourful yet colourless that I am,
Above the ground that I am,
Below the ground that I am,
Around the world that I am,
Storms and calms are my shadows,
Water, water, water, that's what I am.

Shivani Shah (11)
North Bridge House School

Detention

I sit at a desk
With no one to talk to
Except my pen and paper
My breath still smelt
Of the criminal offence
I must not chew gum,
I must not chew gum.

Those words ringing
Through my head.
As my pen scratches
Along the paper
I think to myself . . .
I should definitely
Not chew gum!

India Browne Wilkinson (11)
North Bridge House School

Of Cape Trafalgar

The guns are blazing,
The other ship's bow raising,
That is a clear shot hole.
The T-formation done its role,
The bow is lowering again,
The ship is clearly sunk.

The other ships are coming,
The French are even ramming,
Some of them are fleeing,
We are not even knowing,
That Nelson is now shot.

There was a sudden silence,
It really made no sense.
Then the flagships signalled,
The officers around me
They told me what they read,
Which was that Nelson is now dead.

The French ensigns are lowering,
The last guns have stopped firing,
The men on deck are cheering,
The victory is written
In our history books.

Moritz Hellmich (11)
North Bridge House School

The Mask

Every day she wears a mask
But you can't see it
Because it's she who wears it
It's invisible to the naked eye
You need to look deeper
Into her eyes
'The windows of her soul'
To see what she really thinks of you.

You don't know the real girl
Sometimes she even forgets her
Masks can make her look
Or even feel different
But nobody knows the real girl
Or the secrets she covers with her mask.

Nobody knows what she's thinking about
No one knows her pain
She feels so alone
She covers up feelings, emotions
And this is a terrible thing to keep bottled up,
So dangerous, but she continues to conceal
Everything hidden behind her veil
Her mask.

Venetia Stefanon (14)
North Bridge House School

Red-Tailed Hawk

R ipping rodent limb by limb it will kill it in two seconds,
E xceptional bird of prey.
D aring animal sacrificing itself for food.

T alons as sharp as knives,
A ttacking fast as lightning,
I ntelligent with its prey,
L iking every piece it eats or rips apart,
E yes look out like watching towers,
D eath awaits its opponent.

H unting day and night for food,
A head of its enemy it will kill its future food,
W ith enthusiasm to kill its enemy,
K illing meat for food.

Daniel McKeever-Crowcroft (10)
North Bridge House School

The Tiger

As he runs along
The rough, green ground
Chasing a deer
Who runs around.

The tiger chases
Powerful and weaving
The deer is ahead
Terrified, bleeding.

The tiger pounces
To catch its prey
The deer dodges
And runs away.

Julius Judah (11)
North Bridge House School

Autumn

Autumn is the time when the leaves start falling
And the trees start calling
It's autumn, its autumn!
The trees go bare
And the ground forms a layer of leaves on top of it.
The weather gets colder
And you feel a brisk cold gust of wind fly over your shoulder.
It's such a shame when the rain starts to fall from the sky.
The sky gets greyer
And there is a great change from summer.
The days get shorter and the nights get longer.
Most people love the leaves
The red leaves of autumn,
The leaves keep changing colours every day
And guess what's next, it's winter!

Oliver Newman (11)
North Bridge House School

Untitled Island

An enchanted mirage of isolated beauty
Untouched by man
Blooming in the azure sea
I flourish unnoticed
I'm trapped in a surreal world
Away from humanity, yet not from life
A pinprick on a map
A nothing in the world.

Bright corals glimmer in the sea like jewels
Garlands of tropical flowers drape me
Like a goddess wild fragrances spill round me
My hot breath pulsates
Savage storms break over me
But I remain.

Georgia Mackenzie (13)
North Bridge House School

Blood On The Carpet

The room was quiet and as still as a mouse,
But in her mind the screams still echoed round the house,
Unbearable was the stillness and the quietness,
Worse was her weakness and her loneliness.

Something was lurking in the back of her brain,
Her anxiety and her sweating was driving her insane,
It was cold, freezing,
She was shivering, crying
Intimidation, rejection
And worst of all isolation.

She knew that there would be no escape when a
Key went in the door,
She knew that there would be questions about
The blood all over the floor.

She could not stand her violence,
She could not stand the silence,
Her heart was breaking
Her whole body was quaking
And she could take no more,
She took her life,
And she was right,
When the key went in the door,
There were a lot of questions about
The blood all over the floor.

Natalie Mallin (13)
North Bridge House School

Beauty And The Beast

A mighty roar
Thundered.
The island trembled in the monster's wake.
A galloping soul, a fearsome creature
Proud and tall.
Sniffing . . .
Glaring . . .
Listening . . .
For souls,
It searches, relentless,
Like a tormented man
Looking for a lost dream.
It is, though, a charmer
Of trick and seduction.
A mirage of mirages, a secret of lies.
This Beauty is a Beast.
It glides and skimmers above the lands
Watching with its unpredictable eye
Tempting
Tempting
With its Beauty undoing their sight
Innocent playful this is Beauty with
Its inner Beast.

It is but the tale of Beauty and Beast.

Tariq El Gazzar (13)
North Bridge House School

The Sharks

A fin breaks the placid surface.
The sinuous black body
Weaves in and out of the waves.

Sleek but deadly,
Beautiful but monstrous.
A dolphin? No.
This is the spawn of Satan, the Devil's imp,
The apostate of death.
Its back glistens in the moonlight,
Naked to the sea, just swimming there.

Another fin arises,
Bigger than the other,
Faster and seemingly more savage.
It tilts its head back,
Revealing rows upon rows of -
What?
Could you call them teeth?
They are like a thousand rapiers
Ready to rip into your skin,
Each one flecked with a crimson sludge.

Oh and that mouth,
A never-ending chasm of doom and destruction,
Gaping and wide as a row of buses.

But the eyes,
The eyes are the worst,
Blank and unseeing,
Until they bite you, and the sea is full of red.

And another fin comes,
And another and another.
Soon the water is a seething, boiling mass of sharks.
These abominations of their creator
Ploughing the waves like some death ship.
Torrents of bubbles fly from beneath.
Foam spews out, from the placid surface
That is no more.

Jonathan Birkett (12)
North Bridge House School

The Blackbird

In my short life, I flew over river, roof and hilltop high,
Gliding, swooping, cutting through the air, majestic and fair.

The spring came and with it life, life all-surrounding and embracing,
bursting, rich
A handsome chick born from majestic sleek parents.

In my short life, I remember my first flight; jump, jump
Fly, come, come my mother's words encouraging me on,
With fear I heard my father's distant song,
My fight was on, my pride strong, my love of freedom born.

In my short life, my song was that of my father,
Strong, wonderful and long
The summer, winter come and gone.

Hear me on a summer eve,
Hear me on a winter morn,
Remember another blackbird born.

Think not of my body lying there motorists passing without care
Struck down in mid-flight, I fell like a bullet from the sky,
Left there on that cold, bleak road to die,
With not a helping hand I knew the end was nigh,
I knew this was the end of my flight, the end of my life.

Think of me on a midsummer night,
See another blackbird in flight
Think of life's gift of song, feather, beauty, love and might
Think of rebirth and life.

Take your flight, take your might, seize it now
Without fright, let your spirit take flight.

Another rebirth, another chick like me, a beauty for you all to see,
Another spirit flying free,
Another blackbird just like me.

Charlotte Thompson (15)
North Bridge House School

Untitled

Painful numbness - no one feels it,
Their heads are throbbing,
They can't work it out.

Reality: stop hitting me
Ambitions: stop failing me.

'In the future everything will work out'

Sick of this sarcastic happiness
Nothing is precious
Nothing is delicate
'Smile and everything will be *fine*.'

Isolation is a joke

This silence is killing me -
Cynically trickling up my spine

Stop being borderline,
Dismiss your failure by laughing,
Nothing is reality (Blank)
Emptiness . . . somehow stop overwhelming me,
Nothing is lost.

No one understands,
Why this emotion is overdone.

Amaryllis Garland (14)
North Bridge House School

Staring

I sit staring at the blank white page
My pen poised.
But the ink won't flow,
My ideas are frozen,
Like a man whose feet are locked in deep snow.

The whiteness of the page is blinding.
The challenge it sets too great,
A head full of words,
But none seem right,
What does it take for the idea to ignite?

I stare out of my window for some inspiration,
The sunlight glitters off the swaying leaves,
Everything stands still waiting for the one,
The tidal wave of ideas,
But it seems it will never come.

I think I'll try again later,
When the ink may flow more free,
The ideas might come quickly,
My pen unable to stop,
Until then, I'll give up and go to the shop.

Max Murdy-Flisher (14)
North Bridge House School

The Tragic Tale Of Liposuction

In a world so tough, what is a friend?
A companion with advice and an ear to lend?

You don't always have to show them affection,
Sometimes they can be the object of your rejection.

Sometimes you can use them for personal gain,
This technique usually comes with a sideline of pain.

But when your friend calls for urgent advice,
It can be something serious like going under the knife.

You poke fun when all they want is a weight reduction,
Your cruelty can make them feel a sense of corruption.

But when something tragic happens to them,
You feel bad because you weren't there to the end.

Who would have guessed death would come into action,
While a friend was experiencing liposuction?

Daniel Townsend (14)
North Bridge House School

Ode To The Sea

As freezing waves flung against my feet
I contemplated whether to immerse myself
In the chilling curves
Of the wild waters.
Surrounded by the elements.
Just me and them.
I, used to the urban jungle, find elements free.

As I watch strangers plunge themselves into the sea
I think, *why I cannot do the same*, fear of letting go, civilisation?
When will I be free!

Free, from burdens of self-consciousness,
Free, from the burdens of uncertainty,
Free, from the burden of society.

Will I ever be free?

Lucilla Braune (15)
North Bridge House School

The Beast

The howling of the wind
Could be heard across the desolate landscape.

The beast arose,
Its rage, swelling and swelling,
Ever so silently, ever so slyly,
Casting an everlasting shadow over all humanity.

Its smell suffocating me wherever I walked,
I watched in horror
As it grew ever more hideous,
Twisting, turning, destroying,
Never stopping to think.

It loomed over me,
Getting closer by the second.
I sat there in a trance looking up at it.
I closed my eyes and dreamt of
Foreign lands,
Where I had come from,
My home.

And for a second
In all the chaos and
Commotion
I was free.

But as I opened my eyes
It was too late
I was devoured
By the beast,
The beast, which is this corrupt democracy.

John Shurety (15)
North Bridge House School

Hell's Summer Skies

Men at arms gaze with awe,
Enemy lines remain forthcoming,
Outnumbered, outgunned,
Raining bullets with blare,
Blazing blood and thunder.

All eyes now remain in the skies,
For help, hope, horse power,
Some on their knees, hands out blooming -
Like a rose ablaze,
This was Hell's summer skies.

Unforeseen fate, mélange in the air
To the bloodshot eye, a hawk zooms above
Dropping a nuclear disaster, to
Melt the skies, as the morning melee
Ends, autumn begins.

Alexander Robertson (15)
North Bridge House School

Mankind's Genesis

Evolution of humanity spawned an amorous desire,
To obtain immense, detrimental dominance.
Malice grew within and elaborated,
The result was a weapon beyond imagination,
Mortality's creation brought vast destruction.

Hell erupted and unleashed its ferocious wrath,
A fiery frenzy annihilating all adversaries,
A scorching, smouldering tempest eradicated all existence,
Suffering, pain and decease flooded the entire Earth.

Nothing remained of the corrupted planet,
Only the scar of Satan's kiss.

Darius Anvarzadeh (13)
North Bridge House School

One Mile

Lush green grass.
Laughing, children and adults alike;
Playing football beneath the sweltering sunshine.
The smell of summer roams through the air,
With a sweet, sticky sensation.

Dark alleyways,
Sewage covered floors
Dark, shifty men lurking,
Within the shadows
Like ghosts coming to play.
The smell of corrosion and death,
Hit you with a sting.

A road that links these two
Opposing cultures,
Is filled with men and women,
Coming, back and forth from work.
With children coming to school,
Crossing this warpath, innocently.

Only one mile separates,
Dark, deserted, drug-ridden corners,
With children's swings,
Candy covered parks.

One mile.

Josh Yentob (15)
North Bridge House School

Forgotten Children

We sit in what is left of our home crying,
Wishing it would end
Explosions are everywhere,
Death is near, we can feel it,
A playground once filled with happiness is a smoking crater,
We are the forgotten children of Kosovo.

We are huddling in our school terrified,
Fearing what might happen next,
Gunshots can be heard,
Death is here, we can see it,
A girl once filled with joy is lying dead on the floor,
We are the forgotten children of Palestine.

We are lying in the street starving,
Wondering if there is a better world out there,
Screams reverberating in our heads,
Death has been here, it has touched us,
Our parents once filled with love were executed in front of us,
We are the forgotten children of Afghanistan.

We are the forgotten children of the world.

Paul Smith (13)
North Bridge House School

Continents

Europe the most diminutive of them all
Still the calibre of the cities
Is exasperating.

Asia the sandy relentless wilderness,
The poor grimy smut of the
Villages is unreal.

Australasia, a miraculously alluring
place with tremendous heat.

North America the domineering powerful
Continent. The tyrannical capital
Washington DC.

South America to the west of the azure Atlantic
Ocean. The Andes, the continents
Vertebrae.

Africa with devastating food shortage
That has brought life's every
Cursory end.

Stefan Dockx Xavier (13)
North Bridge House School

The Eye

The grimy world beneath our feet,
Is an endless tunnel,
It is a twisted planet, but without deserts, mountains or beaches,
Its land is the grit, soil and grime that rotate over time.

Filth and impure water flows here,
Mud oozes from holes and through cracks,
Earthquakes plan their very eruptions,
All in one small planet.

Above this universe, where there is solid ground,
Dust swirls and scatters, it sifts through emerald forests,
And aquatic waters, it flutters through golden fields,
It sees everything.

But to travel into space,
The Earth could mimic,
A precious gem,
Swirled with white and blotches of bluish green,

It is the eye of the universe.

Juliet McNelly (12)
North Bridge House School

All In Me

Lying on the floor
Inside an empty room
Silence,
Is all I hear.

Except the screams
Of chaos and violence deep inside,
Raging to come out,
Strangling and choking me.

Llewe Leong (13)
North Bridge House School

A Fallen Angel

Tender tears fall to Hell, within rain's rhythm
A haggard girl slips towards the iciness of marble floors
The warmth of all innocence, dissolved
Is she receiving love?
Yes
Does she know?
No
Too blinded with fear and rejection to use her sight.

The keen, jagged knife, a stranger to her delicate ashen skin.

A distorted shape of figures torment her night and day
The mirror of truth lies to her. Mislead her
Beauty lies within. Yet angels do not know.

Red petals of blood garland her wrist
Rosy dewdrops fall.
With every drop, she does not exist.

A fallen angel, she was.

Ayumi Shimizu (15)
North Bridge House School

Autumn Poem

The golden leaves falling in the cold autumn air,
Hallowe'en comes upon us, witches' fingers, ghosts
and goblins, full moons, werewolves, toffee apples,
trick or treating are all around.
The smells of Bonfire Night waft in the breeze,
The fireworks shoot up in an array of colours,
Filling the night sky.
The crisp sound of dead leaves where people walk,
the windy, short days come and go so swiftly,
The different colours are all around,
the night of Guy Fawkes is when we remember
The gunpowder treason and plot.

Lydia Waldouck (11)
Notting Hill & Ealing High School

Feather Boy

He drifts from place to place,
The harsh wind of peers blowing him away,
Not wanting to show his face,
Being brought down to earth by their words.

In lessons, he's fine,
'Clever boy, that John,'
'Oi, what's the answer to number nine?'
His mind floats in a world of maths and science.

At break he plunges back down to earth,
The delicate white feather is trampled,
Harsh boys flatten him with their taunts,
Leaving him alone, crushed to a pulp.

What did he ever do to them?
Nothing, that's the dreadful crime,
The others tease him, taunt him, exclude him,
For being strange, weird, different.

One day, maybe he can leave,
Float away from this pain and torment,
Drop into a place of happiness and peace,
Where he can float and dream for evermore.

Olivia Williams (13)
Notting Hill & Ealing High School

Autumn

Autumn, when the wind blows strong,
Whistling, writhing, walloping wind,
Battling with his companion, rain . . .
That's how I think of autumn.

Autumn, when car lights shine through thick fog,
Christmas fairy lights sparkle in windows
And the icy frost gleams and sparkles,
That's how I think of autumn.

The taste of apple crumble,
Roast beef and such
And beautifully polished brown conkers . . .
That's how I think of autumn.

The smell of ice, beef
And roast chestnuts,
Of all things typically autumn . . .
That's how I think of autumn.

The forgotten season, in the midst of Christmas,
A brilliant season, with treats in store,
All-hallows tide, Diwali, etc, etc, etc . . .
That's how I think of autumn.

Sophie Shawdon (11)
Notting Hill & Ealing High School

Autumn

The leaves fall,
The animals crawl,
Into hibernation.

The warm food,
A darker mood,
As autumn draws near.

The clocks go back,
Time to get out your umbrella and mac,
As the rain, snow and wind come.

Warm food; apple pie,
As we watch the birds fly
Towards Africa for migration.

Longer nights, shorter days,
As the sun's rays
Disappear at 4 o'clock.

Trudging to school with a laden bag
With the harvest food we drag,
To give to homeless people who need it.

As the conkers fall off the tree
And I see
Their shiny contents.

The summer is gone
And autumn is long
But let's enjoy it while it lasts.

Rosie Owen (11)
Notting Hill & Ealing High School

Autumn Is Here!

Season of falling leaves,
Dead after summer,
Of bonfires and kettles,
Warm to the touch.

Toasted marshmallows
Dripping down their sticks
And fireworks exploding
With multicoloured showers.

The rustle of candy-filled bags
And cries of 'Trick or treat?'
The steam and smell of hot
Things to eat.

Scarves, hats and gloves
Are warm delights
And glittering stars
Brighten up the dark nights.

The winding of clocks
And helping the old
And many sleepovers
Where secrets are told.

But what's this all about,
Surely you've guessed,
It's the forgotten season,
Which is the best.

Hallowe'en is in store
And Christmas is near,
Yes, you've guessed it,
Autumn is here!

Phoebe Syms (11)
Notting Hill & Ealing High School

Autumn

The trees so golden,
Above carpets of crisp, crunchy leaves,
Children nibbling russet apples,
Stamping on spiky cones,
A scramble for mahogany conkers,
Autumn's harvest!

Seasonal celebration,
Crowds gather around the smoky fires,
Crimson colours stain the sky,
As whirling fireworks reach up high,
Into the chill night sky.

Gusting winds and rain appears,
Mists cling to the hillside,
The nights draw longer,
Pack away the summer clothes,
Embrace the winter!

Catrin Jones (11)
Notting Hill & Ealing High School

Autumn

The cold, crisp nights of autumn follow steaming summer nights,
Under blankets I wish to be, my cold trapped for me.
The leaves are falling off the trees,
Some red, some orange, some green.
Time for conker to ground, the brown shiny things.

I sit alone in my room watching the trees become bare,
It looks as though they're moulting, losing all their hair.
Animals start collecting food ready to hibernate,
When they wake it will be spring, ready to mate.
People starting to wrap up warm and put the heating on,
Days are starting to get shorter, and nights long.

Maya Pillay (11)
Notting Hill & Ealing High School

Autumn Feel

Period of dimness and mature flower,
Close to the brim of the future sunset:
Combining with one to fill with power,
With product of the plants the leaves not kept;
To twine with fruit the greenhouse dwelling,
And load all food with tenderness to the centre;
To expand the damson and round the swelling,
What a pleasant season, hopefully more will enter.

Period of festivals and lengthy celebrations,
Close to furnace with a warm tender roast;
Joining with people to share jubilation,
With food of great richness to endure and toast;
To bend with colour the cool robes show,
And load all dishes with warmth to the centre;
To enrich the feeling and let all know,
What a pleasant season hopefully more will enter.

Katy Webb (11)
Notting Hill & Ealing High School

Autumn

I'm forgotten, I'm alone, pushed out of people's minds,
They talk about summer,
They talk about Christmas,
They don't notice me.

I make the mist, frost, fog and rain,
But they don't realise me, again.
I make the leaves drop, I make light stop,
But all they do is shop.

I'm forgotten, I'm alone, pushed out of people's minds,
They talk of summer,
They talk of Christmas,
They don't notice me.
But I'm autumn,
With my golden beauty.

Kate Sheard (12)
Notting Hill & Ealing High School

Dear Autumn

You are the most beautiful season,
Full of all different colours.
You are the season of art.
The season where I stare and stare
And never get bored.

The season for happiness and festival,
You are when I celebrate Diwali,
You are when we Indians celebrate Ram coming back,
The season where we light fireworks.
We have fun and laughter surrounding us,
Wherever you go just light and brightness.
You are the sign of *joy* for us.

With you we play in the leaves
And scare mums by hiding in the leaves.
We feel the lovely leaves gently falling on us,
The slightly cold wind passing by
And at night snuggling in our beds.

You are truly the prettiest,
And when it's time for you to go,
We have sadness and bare trees,
I remember you a lot and wait
For the next year to bring back your colours.

Rukmani Raheja (11)
Notting Hill & Ealing High School

An Autumn Day

They're coming down in showers,
the leaves are all gold and red,
covering the little flowers,
and tucking them in bed.
They've spread a fairy carpet
all up and down the street
and when we skip to school,
they rustle under our feet.

Pumpkins in the fields,
gold around the brown,
leaves of rust and scarlet
trembling slowly down.
Birds travel southward,
lovely time to play,
nothing is as pleasant
as an autumn day!

When the trees have a splendid
summer they change to raiment red and gold.
When the summer moon turns mellow
and the nights are getting cold,
while the squirrels hide their acorns
but nothing is as pleasant
as an autumn day!

Sailaja Suresh (11)
Notting Hill & Ealing High School

The Gentle, The Sweet

Autumn is a time of farewell,
When birds migrate and
Animals hibernate.
Days get colder, swirling mist,
Dark, dense nights. The gentle, the sweet.

Deserted mornings. The breeze
Clears the night away leaving
Spiderwebs glistening with crystal dew.
The dying gloom, the baby day.

Leaves cascading, tinged with
Russet, ochre, flame they flutter
From the crest of the tree piling up
In mountains tall, brittle to the touch.

Animals forage for acorns hard or
Succulent, crimson berries. Mushroom'
Cushions sprout from the musty soil,
Delicate or meaty.

Bonfires crackle, their tongues licking
Golden sticks. The smoke wafts into
The air coating the grass with ashes.

Twilight comes with crescent moon.
Pricks of light like glass shards
Sprinkled here and there.
Chill air dances in
Shimmering like a lake.

Autumn is a time of farewell,
When birds migrate and
Animals hibernate.
Days get colder. Swirling mist,
Dark, dense nights. The gentle, the sweet.

Alice Kent (11)
Notting Hill & Ealing High School

Memories

Sit.
Come and think of all the joys you had,
Think of all the pleasant times,
The hopes and thoughts and all the dreams,
The cheerful carefreeness of life.

Memories will last for eternity,
Remember that, and more.
For photos fade and pictures go,
But memories never stray.

Think of the good days, and the bad,
The days that made you cry,
Think of them as jewels, my friend,
'Cause memories will not die.

Think of times when you grew up,
Those happy childhood days.
When trouble and fear were both unknown,
And you had all your dreams.

Remember when you could not cry,
When time was bad and hope was gone,
Forget not those days, for they will stay,
Beside you until the end.

Look back and remember love,
As if it still were here,
Now rest awhile and think again,
Of everything you've seen.

Catherine Hall (17)
Notting Hill & Ealing High School

The Lonely Season

The leaves on the trees are falling,
The sun is never dawning,
Never a bright morning,
Because it's the lonely season.

The insects are all crawling,
The mammals are all yawning,
To get away from the rain that is sprawling,
Because it's the lonely season.

All the people are yearning,
The sun that used to be burning,
Always bushes cowering,
Because it's the lonely season.

Guy Fawkes is really firing,
Hallowe'en is very frightening,
Trouble has been stirring,
Because it's the lonely season.

Isabel Spanswick (11)
Notting Hill & Ealing High School

An Autumn Poem

Trees covered in golden leaves,
Swaying gently with the breeze.
Shorter days and longer nights,
Soon the birds will take their flights.

Conkers scattered on the ground,
Spiky, golden, brown and round.
Car lights turning on,
As the day is nearly gone.

Morning mist and evening fog,
Urban cities drenched in smog.
Rain is falling everywhere,
Now that autumn is finally here.

Katie Healey (12)
Notting Hill & Ealing High School

Autumn

I am the forgotten season,
the one that's always left out.
All I want to do is cry and shout,
To grab attention, to show off my leaves and rain,
So I cry my eyes out as I am in pain.
I cry over people's windscreens but,
they just wipe me off.
I drop my leaves onto the ground,
they get stepped on and that is so tough!
So, how can I prevent my pain?
Is it by rain all over again?
It can't be!
It does haunt me,
To think that I am the forgotten season.
I shall go on a hunt,
to find my fame, all over again.

Anita Foroshani (11)
Notting Hill & Ealing High School

Autumn, The Forgotten Season

Autumn, the forgotten season,
Let's see, where should I start?
The red, the orange, the yellow,
It's a living piece of art.
The fog and frost in the morning,
The warm evenings at home.
Squirrels out on your doorstep,
So you'll never be alone.

The first day of school is in autumn,
So it's bye-bye to the holidays,
But autumn couldn't be better,
It's a season waiting to come.
So next time, please don't ignore it,
Because it's a season pretty and fun.

Tula Nansi (11)
Notting Hill & Ealing High School

Metropolis

Wave after wave of figures
Sweep through the streets
In a never-ending sea of colour, size and shape.
Neon bright, blinding signs
Shimmer, howl and grin,
Enticing passers-by.
Brightly lit doorways
Fling shafts of light
Across the street
Like gleaming arrows
From an invisible bow.
And the people, packed in tight
Struggle like too many fish
Caught in a net
Shoving, fighting, gasping for air.
Many are forced against the dripping walls
To cower and watch the surge
Sometimes tumbling into darkened alleys
To be swallowed helplessly in the blackness.
The stars have long been chased from the sky
Leaving mankind to choke and splutter
On their own polluted air.
The skyscrapers prick the heavens
And the night's blood ricochets off the garish tarpaulins,
As the mannequins in the shop window
Smile vacantly down.
The city by night.

Anna Reid (12)
Notting Hill & Ealing High School

Blood Sports

'Twas a lovely day to hunt foxes,
We saddled up the horses
And called out with the hounds,
Wiped the blood from our hands
On our nannies' pinnies,
Our hunting pink jackets cost ninety guineas
Which are a shilling each more
Than poor people's pounds.

Today I'll go badger baiting
For all the winter they've been mating
Surely the set won't miss a few
So we'll break their little backs,
Let the dogs from the sacks
And cheer as the blood spurts
On me and on you.

The third of each month is hare coursing day,
My fine young lurchers relish the chase,
Their prey's bug eyes will fill with fear,
We'll all salute at the blood and guts
And envy the jaws and teeth of the mutts,
As they taste the death and hear the last breath.
We have to settle for a well-earned beer.

Sophie Baker (17)
Notting Hill & Ealing High School

Echoes Of Autumn

Red, orange and yellow leaves fall from the darkening sky.
My hands toasty warm in my bright mittens.
Roasted chestnuts baking in my pocket,
And the swallows migrate to a faraway land.

Blazing bonfires lying on their bed of sticks,
Clutching a Guy Fawkes close to my chest,
Ready to plunge him into the licking flames.
And stars appear like freckles in the moonlit emptiness.

Wheels of fire dance on their posts,
Coloured rockets soar into the frosty air.
My flaring sparkler burns with joy,
And the cackle of fireworks echo in the misty sky.

The wet leaves lie at the bottom of trunks,
While the bare body of the trees wave in the wind.
My breath hangs in the air like smoke,
And my vapour swoops away.

Georgia Posner (11)
Notting Hill & Ealing High School

Good Morning Autumn

Good morning Autumn,
And how are you?
I haven't seen you for a while,
Don't forget to bring . . .

Your orange leaves and conkers falling,
Clocks going back in time,
Hallowe'en and harvest coming,
Thanksgiving too,
Fireworks darting here and there through the sky of the night,
Bonfires in gardens lighting up excited faces as they watch,
The rich and ripe colours (which every year you bring)
The cosy evenings and warm food that we all enjoy,
Rain and frost, wind and mist,
Longer nights for me to sleep.

Jess Taylor (11)
Notting Hill & Ealing High School

Why?

Why did you have to go?
It wasn't time, it wasn't so.

You didn't have to leave,
I didn't wanna believe.

It's all gone bare
When you haven't been there.

Loneliness races around
Thinking of you makes me cry and fall to the ground.

Your laugh, your smile,
When I was a child.

Memories are all that is left,
To me you are the best.

All the tears I cry,
I always wonder why!

Gemma Dybell
Phoenix High School

Description

If this person was furniture,
He would be an armchair.
If this person was an adjective,
He would be calm.
If this person was clothing,
He would be a suit.
This person is a sports fan,
He loves football,
He loves to play,
But now he is a bit older,
Instead he teaches English now,
And that's a relief for us.

Ariunzaya Bazarsad (12)
Phoenix High School

Crossroad

It was at the funeral where it all began,
you don't have to pay transmission from a boy to a man,
lost sight of my mother at the age of nine,
didn't understand death, nearly lost my mind.
My dad turned to the bottle every time he was sad,
I missed her so much I wanted her bad.
At the age of ten, I was taken away from my father,
separated from my family except for my brother.
We were taken to a new family which wasn't my own,
my brother and I were so alone, all my brother did was
                                    shout and moan.
I was taken in by the gang from the estate,
we got into trouble, so I thought it was my fate.
I felt like I was in a room with no windows but a locked gate,
full of trouble, each day it got worse it felt like double.
Then I started thinking, *where is all this trouble getting me?*
Just all these people pestering me.
I put my head into the books and got an A,
I knew this was right so I wasn't heading the wrong way.
I left school with a few GCSEs, so if I was bad I'd be begging
                                    on my knees,
then I got a new house with my own keys.
I thought about my mum and said, 'Goodbye,'
Walked into my new home with my head held high.

Marlon Modeste (14)
Phoenix High School

A History Lesson

The clock is ticking, ticking away,
Each tick seems like more than a day,
The stones in the cage don't want to stay,
Yet none of them know what is causing this delay.

The ink on the page is hypnotising us,
It makes us think about the fun on the bus,
It's there that all of us speak, fight and cuss,
Everything happens there to use up all our lust.

Something happens now, in the blinding light,
Some kids in a PE lesson just begin to fight,
The class rushes out and even I just might,
If I wasn't caught by the teacher's fearsome bite.

Instantly the head is called to calm everyone down,
When he gets to the edge of it, we all can feel his frown,
For what was once a lively green has turned to muddy brown,
The fight ceases when all see the head's almighty crown.

The bell begins to ring,
The children start to sing,
The teacher is no longer king,
The bags we forget to bring.

Now that the day is done,
We can all shout and run,
Missing bags hit us like a ton,
We return to the place of no fun,
And later come back to the sun.

Joseph Cotter (14)
Phoenix High School

It

It's not easy being a thing called 'it',
Especially when your own mother has given you the status.
Do you know what it feels like to be so graciously loved,
Then ripped from that source of love?
To be ripped of all status,
To be the thing known as 'it'?
Well, let me tell you,
I no longer have a purpose for existence,
I no longer know night from day,
I no longer know stench from perfume,
I no longer know Heaven from Hell.
What I do know,
What I am definitely certain of
Is that I will forever rot in the state of gloom,
Without receiving love or giving love,
And my body shall lie in the temple of doom.

Nyasha Thomas (14)
Phoenix High School

The Wish Of The Star

I saw the star twinkle at me,
Down came the light and surrounded me.

As I looked up and saw a shooting star,
I was so dizzy, I saw flying cars.

The star said in a squeaky voice,
'Hey, little girl, let me hear your voice.'

I started to shake with lots of fear,
But the star was just standing drinking beer.

But now it's time for the star to go,
'Bye-bye little girl, I must go and roam.'

Kaliegh Gilbert (11)
Phoenix High School

Bullies, Bullies Who Bully Me

Bullies, bullies
Bully me,
I hate these bullies
Who bully me.
Tell those bullies
To stop bullying me
And tell my mum
They're bullying me.

Help these bullies
Who bully me,
Stop them from
Bullying me,
Tell the teacher
They bully me
And tell my mum,
'Stop crying for me.'

Shenika Brown-Wilson (13)
Phoenix High School

Grandad

I remember the way he used to sit in his chair
Reading the paper without a care,
Him doing the crossword, with whisky in hand,
To me he was the greatest man throughout the land.
His love of gardening and knowledge of plants
Inspiring me always.
His cupboard full of sweets and games, just for me,
And his Sunday dinner, the best that you could see,
His knowledge and brains, my greatest inspiration.
What a brilliant man, my grandad.

Sarah Militello (14)
Phoenix High School

It's My First Day

I woke up and got dressed
As a confident five-year-old.
We left the house
With my heart full of gold.

I stood at the main gate
Shaking in my shoes,
I did not know what school would be like,
I wanted some clues.

When I went inside,
I saw a kid,
His hat was shaped
Like it was a lid.

My teacher was tall,
She was nice,
My school was old,
It had some mice.

We all played with toys,
It was great fun,
I didn't stop playing
With the big gun.

At the end of the day,
I had learned many things,
As I left the school,
My heart began to sing.

Murdhanya Dave (14)
Phoenix High School

Reality

Life starts with a shiny painful light,
Which beams into your eyes.
It hurts more than a car hitting you
Because it is the first time you see such a thing.
You cry, to show them you are suffering
So then they take you in their arms and comfort you.
You have now opened your eyes.

A few years go by,
You can walk and talk
But there are some things you must learn
Before you step into the outside world.
You will never know what they will expect from you
And you will never know what you will expect from them.
Watch your back!

So far, so good.
You have got friends now
But is that a good thing?
If it is, will you protect them
Or will they protect you?
You will see soon.
Just watch your back!

Finally you're out.
Having fun?
Going home after an energetic night
You pass a few blocks,
Mysterious shadows in front of you.
You feel cold, then you see the light.
You have now closed your eyes.
I told you to watch your back!

Nashir Uddin (14)
Phoenix High School

Miss Picky

However good your work is,
However neat the page,
It won't escape Miss Picky
In a criticising rage.

'I'm only marking like an examiner would,'
Is probably her favourite phrase,
The last time she complimented me
Seems like a foggy haze!

The words don't seem to matter,
The only things that count
Are written very neatly
And never crossed out!

So how will I live with this?
Just think it's obvious, dude,
In two years' time
You won't have to put up with her mood!

Imam Quadir (14)
Phoenix High School

Summer Holiday

Sun, sand and frolics in the sea
Shorts, bikini and sunbathing
Beach bums and surf enthusiasts
Beach parties, music, drugs and sex
Summer love, broken hearts and regrets
Tears, laughter and new friends
But the best thing about summer
Is what you've learnt and experienced.

Ifrah Jeylani (15)
Phoenix High School

Freedom!

When the sky is green
and the grass is blue,
that's when the world will tell the truth.

People will try,
children will cry
but do they know the world will die?

Poverty and criminals
strip the Earth of its glory.
Should we sit tight
or should we kill and worry?

When the lion is found
lying next to her baby,
then maybe, just maybe
if we listen we can hear them
and then one day the Earth will cry
Freedom!

Hannah Cadir (15)
Phoenix High School

The Movements Of The Night

The trees howl and sway in the wind,
The shadows fall upon the ground,
The cars go past on the motorway
As the lorries honk their horns.
I hear thunder rumble in the distance
And the crack of lightning,
I snuggle up in my duvet
Hoping the rays of the sun
Will come and bring a new day.

Ayan Yusuf (11)
Phoenix High School

Gone Was The Time

Gone was the time
when we used to smile at each other
and we used to sit in class together,
laughing out loud at our own jokes together.

Gone was the time
we did our homework in hiding
and we used to do our own dividing
listening to my brother doing his vibing.

Gone was the time
we used to party till eight
and we used to stay up till late
watching videos like it was a faith.

Gone was the time
used to look in your eyes looking startled,
then we started to grow thinking I was baffled
until I got to the day I had to say, 'I love you.'

Ian Barnor (15)
Phoenix High School

The Sun

With a pleasant smile
It rises to the dark sky
Lighting up every square mile
Going high and high.

Covering everything with her numerous arms
Cuddling the Earth like mother and child,
Greeting her fellow sky mates with open arms,
Their gatherings are often wild,
Resulting in a brighter, sunnier day.

Nadifa Ahmed (11)
Phoenix High School

That Voice

As that echo reverberates in my ear,
I become bright like a glowing light,
The brightness makes me feel good,
Good as the smell of Blue Jeans.

That voice makes me go to sleep,
When I hear it in the morning, I feel awake
Because it is better than an alarm clock,
That's why I say, 'That voice.'

That voice brings me success,
Success that makes me feel happy,
Happiness that makes me feel good,
That's why I say, 'That voice.'

That voice, I hope, will always be there for me,
It brings good things,
It brings happiness,
It brings success.

Andrew Larbi (15)
Phoenix High School

Flowers

F is for the flowing breeze,
L is for the lovely trees
O is for the oriental flowers,
W is for the wonderful white roses,
E is for the evening glow,
R is for the red, red roses,
S is for the sunny sunflowers.

Rachel Graver (12)
Phoenix High School

I Thought I Had Life Figured Out

I thought I had life figured out
I had thought about the future and done with the past
Then somebody came back
And then I knew what I had could never last.

Life since they came has gone wrong
Foes became friends and friends became foes
Close friends I knew stopped telling the truth
I feel like an arrow that's been shot with a bow.

Since they came back nothing is right
My world is now inclement and hazy
They had no reason to come back
Please go, please I'm going crazy.

I thought I had life figured out
But now they're all up in my business.
I've made it this far without them
Maybe you can help and guess who it is?

Kenisha Cooke-Weir (13)
Phoenix High School

Memories

I close my eyes and think of times that have all gone,
and past birthday parties, Christmases and times that never last.
But in my head are memories that belong to me alone,
and when I'm sad I close my eyes and think of the past,
but now I see that memories mean more to me than words.
They're images that I will take with me and know that they will last.

Jade McElligott (13)
Phoenix High School

Walk With Me

Hi . . .
I'm seeing a couple of things wrong,
With the way that I'm living,
So come and walk with me.
I just need a second opinion.
I'll introduce you to my friends.
I need to see if you notice
If they're loyal,
Or if they have all got an ulterior motive
I've seen some snakes
With their tails in the door,
Ever since I took drugs,
I don't know what's real anymore.
I'm paranoid, so excuse me
If I seem to be nervous,
But everybody I have killed,
Now they're trying to resurface.
The bottom line is,
I was lonesome,
But I was wrong to do the things I did,
Yeah, I was wrong, son,
I've got issues, but I try
But if I ever get rid of them, I will die.

William Earles (15)
Phoenix High School

Hallowe'en

Hallowe'en's near, Hallowe'en's here,
The time that we play and we scare.
The witches we see on their broomsticks,
The bats that travel in a five or six,
The black cats that stop and stare at you,
The vampires that come out at twelve o two
The kids that come out to trick or treat,
They may ask for money or just a sweet.
The pumpkins that light up at night,
The owls that howl and give you a fright,
The moon that's as big as can be,
The Scream masks that are so scary.
While you're eating a nice roast,
You may happen to see a real ghost.
You might hear a roaring noise, it might be a tiger
Or it might just be a spider.
All the treats that are in your tummy,
Be careful you might spot a walking mummy,
Frankenstein's up, awake from the dead,
Really hungry, looking for bread.
The night's dark and very cold too,
I don't really like Hallowe'en much, do you?

Nicole Phillip (14)
Phoenix High School

The Sparkle Of The Star

As night falls
And the sun goes down,
The moon climbs up
And the stars shine around.

I lay back
With my mum,
The stars had shone
Brighter than the sun.

The darkness
Shaded with the stars,
The shooting stars
Looked like zooming cars.

I looked to my mum
As she snuggled up
And I felt so comfortable
Stroking my pup.

As the day rises
And the moon goes down,
The sun climbs up
And the clouds float around.

Jacqueline Abakah (11)
Phoenix High School

When I Look In Your Eyes

When I look in your eyes,
I see you hiding your pain
You may laugh, but I know you want to cry.

When I look in your eyes,
I see you have had hurt in your life
You can deny, but your eyes can't.

When I look in your eyes,
I see your hopes and dreams
But you look sad, you think you cannot achieve them.

When I look in your eyes,
I see you yearn for love
Go with those boys, trust me they don't love you.

When I look in your eyes,
I see you, the real you
You are just a scared little girl.

But you know, when I look in my eyes
I hate the person I see
Some person I just don't trust.

Sivanna Sherry (13)
Phoenix High School

Time Beyond Us

The stars, the moon, the sun so bright,
Soon will be out of sight.
The future is dark, the future is damp,
Not even an oily lamp.

The sun's flames are burning out,
One by one you couldn't count.
The orange, the red, the yellow, the green,
This is the future I have seen.

Back in time to the ice age again,
The rain, the ice, the cold, the pain.
The water's cold as ice and frozen,
This is the path fate has chosen.

Standing, guarding the gate tall and thin,
Will it let me in?
Its wings, its gown white and long,
Singing a gentle song.

When I entered through a cloud,
I heard not a sound.
When it reached into its gown I clenched a little fist,
Then its hand reappeared, in its hand was a list.

Ticking off names with a golden pen,
Finally it came to the men.
All year long I was there,
Not even moving a hair.

Finally I heard a bell,
I thought I was going to Hell.
Then the thing said, 'Enter,'
I walked into the centre.

Aydrous Yousef (13)
Phoenix High School

Who Is He?

Just feel the skin,
My hands tremble with fear as they stretch for its
Veneer. Who's he to jeer me around?
Just take off its lid; it might be a good - deed
Who's he to jeer me around?
I'm not givin' my eye to its padding if that's what he's
Thinking. Who's he to jeer me around?
My eyes lurch with deep disgust and optimum acrimony
As the balls within the sockets of my eyes
Dart to view the bowels of its thick insides;
My hands clasp over my nose.
His stinking mouth roars with a tumultuously evil laughter.
'Sorry,' I hear him say, as my head bobs and sways.
What a shame to have my hands stitched to its frame;
Only to realise that he who it was is he that I am.

Adolf Bour Jnr (15)
Phoenix High School

What Is Red?

What is red? Roses are red,
Round my garden shed.

What is brown? A tree trunk's brown,
Long and cylindrical.

What is yellow? A lemon's yellow,
Juicy, sour and mellow.

What is white? A seagull's white,
High up in the sky.

What is blue? My wheelchair's blue,
Shining like a sapphire.

What is green? The leaves are green,
Long, pointing and thin.

What is gold? Why gold is gold,
Just gold.

Tasos Kanas (12)
Richard Cloudesley Special School

What Is Gold?

What is gold? My bracelet is gold
Sitting on my wrist.

What is blue? The bin is blue
Standing on the floor.

What is black? Hair is black
When it is my dad's.

What is white? Milk is white
Poured into your tea.

What is red? My door is red
At the front of my house.

What is brown? Chocolate is brown
I love chocolate ice cream with chocolate sauce.

What is grey? Clouds are grey
When it rains.

Gurkan Bozdere (12)
Richard Cloudesley Special School

What Is Red?

What is red? A pear is red
Hanging on its tree.

What is blue? Chelsea are blue
Belting home the ball.

What is silver? The door knob's silver
Turning in my hand.

What is yellow? The Simpsons are yellow
Why you little . . . !

What is green? An emerald's green
Sparkling in the light.

What is gold? A crown is gold
Sitting on its silken pillow.

What is ruby? Why a ruby
Just a ruby.

Luke Hutchins (12)
Richard Cloudesley Special School

What Is Red?

What is red? Blood is red
When you have a cut.

What is blue? A parrot's blue
In the aviary at the zoo.

What is gold? Mum's tooth is gold
Sitting in her mouth.

What is yellow? My folder's yellow
Holding all my work.

What is brown? A box is brown
Sitting on the ground.

What is green? People's hair is green
When they're in the circus.

What is silver? Why silver
Just silver.

Matthew Ellerbeck (13)
Richard Cloudesley Special School

What Is Black?

What is black? The night sky is black
With little yellow stars.

What is grey? A cloud is grey
With raindrops falling from it.

What is brown? Tree trunks are brown,
Leaves like wings and branches like arms.

What is white? Snow is white
Cold and damp when squeezed.

What is peach? Skin is peach,
Soft and pink and furry.

What is multicoloured? A rainbow is multicoloured,
Red and blue and purple.

What is apricot? Why an apricot,
Just an apricot.

Sebahat Cinar (14)
Richard Cloudesley Special School

What Is Snow?

Snow is like a white duvet,
Snow is like a huge, white, blank page,
Snow is like the lovely white clouds in the sky,
Snow is as big as the North Pole.
Snow is the best time of the year!
Snow is as fluffy as a sheep's fur,
Snow brings romance everywhere,
Snow is as fresh as water,
Snow is as white as your teeth,
Snow is as clear as crystals.
Do you like snow?
    I do!

Amandeep Sidhu (11)
Sarah Bonnell School

When I Think Of Love

When I think of love, I think of hearts.
Hearts on my card and hearts on my pillow.
Hearts on my presents and hearts on my CDs.
Hearts to my left and hearts to my right.
Hearts on my face.

When I think of love, I think of red roses.
The colour of love that will make my heart stronger,
Knowing there's someone out there who cares for me.

When I think of love, I think about chocolate.
Chocolate waiting to be eaten by two people in love.
Heart-shaped chocolate sitting by a candlelit dinner.

When I think of love, I think about a romantic dinner.
A dinner with candles, that are so very bright.
Lovely heart-shaped food, waiting to be eaten by two.
Two desserts with a heart-shaped cherry on top.

Luthfa Begum (12)
Sarah Bonnell School

When I Think Of Flowers

When I think of flowers, I think of going on a date.
The man of my dreams will come and give them to me
on my first ever date.
When I think of flowers, I think of a midsummer morning.
The smell of the gentle flowers will fill up my house
with strong, lovely fragrances.
When I think of flowers, I think about roses, red roses
shining so bright, filling my garden with red, red flowers.
When I think of flowers I think of Valentine's Day,
The day that a person will come and give me
a bunch of flowers.

Fahimah Khanom (12)
Sarah Bonnell School

Friendship

Friendship is a priceless gift
That cannot be bought or sold,
Its value is far greater than
An island made of gold.

For gold is cold and lifeless
It can neither see or hear
And in its time of trouble
It's powerless to cheer.

It has no ears to listen
No soul to understand,
It cannot bring you comfort
Or reach out a helping hand.

So when you ask God for a gift
Be thankful for what he sends,
Not diamonds, pearls or riches
But the love of real true friends.

Rachel Roberts (12)
Sarah Bonnell School

Dark And Lonely

It's dark, I'm alone
I can hear the outside world
I can hear rats squeaking

It's dark, I'm alone
I want to go home
But no one loves me.
The water drips day and night.

It's dark, I'm alone
I lay in peace and wait
Till it's my turn to die.

Thelma Simpson (12)
Sarah Bonnell School

My Endless Love

Our love will always forever endure,
Our hearts will be together as I can assure.
My love for you will always be cherished,
Your name in my heart will never be blemished.

Your gentle touch and loving embrace,
Will always remind me of your gorgeous face.
Oh, I would give the world to you,
You are my everything, my sanctuary too.

My love for you will never end,
Your gentle smile will always make my soul bend.
Your tender voice makes my mind comforted,
Your handsome eyes make my soul lofted.

Your sweet little wink makes my heart want to sing,
When I look at you, angelic bells ring.
Everything about you I love so much,
Your smile, your eyes, your gentle touch.

I love you to bits how could I ever leave you?
My heart is yours, your heart is mine,
My love for you will always be divine,
My endless love so fine.

Beatrice Owusu-Ansah (12)
Sarah Bonnell School

What Is Our World?

Our world is not the root of all evil
as it is sometimes unjustly portrayed.
This is done by powerful countries
who are making others gradually fade.

The air has the unmistakable smell of war,
ready to dispose of people who oppose the law.

I ask, is this a world we take pride in,
or just another wonderful place plagued by sin?

Sophie Dar (12)
Sarah Bonnell School

What Was It?

I looked outside the window
I noticed something quaint
It bothered me completely
It looked stressed, maybe it was to faint?

I followed it with patience,
It took me to an alleyway.
Still strange, I saw rose petals
Leading to a balcony.

Still interested I became surrounded,
The scent was surely perfume
It stopped and turned towards me
My heart pumped faster:
Ba-boom, ba-boom, ba-boom.

It stared, it glared and it smiled
I wasn't sure what it was doing
It had hazel-green eyes, sharp and bold
It had a massive puss pimply thing.

It finally turned away
I was thinking: *phew!*
The rose petals led to an abandoned storage place.
It never put its hood down, was it a clue?

It pointed to the ground was it a sign?
I didn't find anything just some rusted steel
I pivoted towards its last position.
It was gone. Was it real?

Senel Akarca (12)
Sarah Bonnell School

You Hurt Me Bad

Love is something so, so pure
When I see you I love you more and more
Each day and night we spend together
Makes me think this will last forever.

But then one night you don't appear
To find that you have disappeared
I sit in my room all alone
Wondering what time you will come home.

I hear a noise it was the door
Was it you I'm really sure
As I opened it I rubbed my eyes
And when I looked up I was so surprised.

It was you, you had come back home
But I found you were not alone
A girl, you were holding hands
Could it be, I don't understand
Was I not good enough, was I that bad
That you had to leave me feeling sad?

Was it an affair, was it a fling
That you had to bring her and me not even a ring?
Now that you have gone
And your life has moved on
I might as well do the same
Even though it's a lot of pain.

Now it's time to say goodbye
As this will be my one last cry
It's time to forgive, it's time to forget
As this is my life I do not regret.

Goodbye my love, goodbye.

Leeacea Robinson (12)
Sarah Bonnell School

Our Declared Love - Romeo And Juliet

Romeo: Oh Juliet for you my heart beats on
Juliet: Romeo your smile surpasses the sun

Romeo: I would for you make every cockerel call your name,
so every listener, a fragment of my joy, they'd gain
Juliet: Not 1,000 painters could capture the beauty I see
in your eyes each day, nor the elegance in the way you dance
and sway

Romeo: My love for you is as everlasting as the evergreen,
when I'm not awake you're present in my dreams.
Juliet: My love for you is as strong as the Scottish mountain tops,
even beyond the grave, unlike our bodies,
our love will never rot.

Rochelle Rodgers (14)
Sarah Bonnell School

Love Is A Four-Letter Word

With passion and fear
Love is a four-letter word
With anger and tears
Love is a four-letter word
When you are with your lover all the time
Love is a four-letter word
When he buys you flowers and you dine
Love is a four-letter word
When he calls your nickname and is on the game
Love is a four-letter word
When love is your aim
Love is a four-letter word
When there is disappointment and heartbreak
Love is a four-letter word
When there is break-up and heartache.

Oluwaseyi Akiwowo (12)
Sarah Bonnell School

Beach Of Sun

In the sun on the beach
People like to relax their feet
Playing around in the sand
Listening to the hard rock band

Swimming in the crystal sea
Looking at all the sights they can see
Eating all the great seafood
Which puts them in a really good mood

Seagulls soaring through the sky
Screeching out with their awful cries
Ponies galloping all around
Making their noisy sounds

People picnicking in the sun
Eating the chicken buns
Kids digging deep in the sand
Working really hard with their hands

Lifeguards making sure everyone's OK
Hope they get a fairly good pay
People all around, having a really good time
No one's committing any crimes

Because Beach of Sun is the greatest place
In all of the human race.

Maegan Sayers (11)
Sarah Bonnell School

Hot Chocolate

This year you will not,
Receive a teddy bear,
Or a satin heart,
My love.

This year,
I will give you hot chocolate,
Not because I don't love you,
But because you are sweet
And beautiful,
It is like our love,
Because you are so joyful and loving.

My gift to you is,
Hot chocolate,
Because it burns
And hurts you if it drops.

Take my gift
And keep it close to your heart,
My gift will always be,
Special to me,
If you hold it tight,
I hope you always,
Keep it to remember,
Our sweet love,
Remember that I will always love you,
Because you are my heart and soul.

Lauren Moynihan (12)
Sarah Bonnell School

No Way Out

This year you will not receive a locket
or a chain
or even flowers.

This year I will give you a maze
because it
symbolises the different pathways we take
and our determination to be together.
It is like our love
because there is no way out,
it's sometimes confusing
or even bemusing.

My gift to you is a maze
because it's overgrown and dark like our love.
Our love is lost
it's challenging and puzzling
and sometimes troubling.
It's like a maze because
there are lots of pathways to take
but you can't always find the right one.

Take my gift and keep it close to your heart.
My gift will always be an emblem of our love
and remember that there's always a way out
if you follow your instincts
and trust your heart.

Lena Ismay (12)
Sarah Bonnell School

Brothers And Sisters

B rothers are annoying but I love them very much
R espect they still give you in a funny manner
O utside they love going
T o play their sporty games
H ate being good boys, like being bad boys.
E very time they are with their mates, you don't want to know them
R espect they like to be given, even if they are smaller than you
S o you don't want to sit with them when they're angry.

A nd only sisters can keep them calm
N othing can stop a girl from being herself
D on't try taking their bag or you're in trouble.

S isters can drive you mad
I n life they are always there
S isters come with their own personalities
T o try and change their personalities would never work
E very time you need them they will always be there
R unning away will never work
S isters are sisters for life but brothers are only brothers
    until they get their wives.

Saffya Yaseen (11)
Sarah Bonnell School

Love

L oving you brings me to ease
O ver the mountains and far away I see you my love
V ery is the word to describe how much I love you
E arth is not big enough for the love I have for you

Y ou are so sweet, sweeter than chocolate
O h every time I see you my heartbeat increases
U ntil the day I set eyes on you, I never felt this way before,
    that's why I'm thanking you today.

Charlie Kaur (15)
Sarah Bonnell School

They Die Not, Who Die For A Good Cause

Accept the reality, respect the reality
They die not, who die for a good cause
Surely! They die not, who die for a good cause

They may not be in this world physical
But they live in our heart, mind and soul
They die not, who die for a good cause,
Surely! They die not, who die for a good cause.

Struggling against the base desires
Fought the evil beings and bad doers
Carrying the burden of mankind on his shoulders
Struggling to survive in the scorching desert
River so close, but yet so far
Seeking for clouds on the sky
Reaching the hearts of all people alive
They die not, who die for a good cause
Surely! They die not, who die for a good cause.

Many dreams have been shattered
Many men have been battered
The game of blood has risen
But! *Thank God for this time*
Many throats sliced but spoke their mind
Reaching the hearts of all people alive
They die not, who die for a good cause
Surely! They die not, who die for a good cause.

The sun by day, the moon at night
Sun, touch, eyes, three kinds of light
Plants, flowers, trees so tall
Roses, lilies, ivy on the wall
Desert, jungles, mountains high
The book of nature, Earth and sky
They die not, who die for a good cause
Surely! They die not, who die for a good cause.

Syeda Fazaila Hussnain Bukhari (12)
Sarah Bonnell School

In The Aeroplane

Up, up, up into the sky I go,
Relaxed in an aeroplane seat,
Left all my games at home, oh no,
So I sit and stare at my feet.

Looking, looking, looking at the sky,
My mind outside the window,
I thought that birds could fly this high,
But really they're down below.

Landing, landing, landing on the ground,
Waiting to get off the plane,
People still sleeping there's hardly a sound,
About to wake up by the sound of the heavy rain.

Amanda Thomas (11)
Sarah Bonnell School

I Wish I Had A Twin

I wish I had a twin
someone like me.
A double, a match
anything the same as me.

We could share gossip and secrets
and play kings and queens.
Even in the bath
we'd get each other clean.

If I get this wish of mine
I'll make a lot of din,
because now I've got a best friend
my very own twin.

Jasmin Ahmed (12)
Sarah Bonnell School

War Is Sadness

When war ends it's sadness
When all of our loved ones die;
It's painful and hurtful
You can't do anything about it
But just cry;
It's like a needle going into your heart
And stuck there forever;
Crying does help forgetting,
It only brings back memories.
When war ends it's sadness
When all our loved ones die;
In six years' time you'll forget about it,
But that type of sadness will never, ever
Go away but it will always be inside your heart,
No matter what you're feeling on the outside.
It won't go away.

Tamzida Pasha (12)
Sarah Bonnell School

A Night's Exit

Everyone fleeing for their life,
People collapsing, unable to move,
Babies crying,
Trees rustling,
Men laughing,
Guns screeching,
People gasping for air,
Jumping at every movement,
Footsteps echoing,
Bodies quivering vigorously
But secure at last,
In a safe place.

Ayaan Ali (11)
Sarah Bonnell School

Shattered World

The world sits still and waits,
As millions bleed every day,
They tell each other things will change,
But the rich remain rich
And the poor remain poor.

Explain to me this,
Why we live in a shattered world?
Everyone is self obsessed and very cold.

Answer me this,
Will our materialistic gain accompany us
To our graves,
Or will the guilt of the nuclear weapons you built,
The innocent lives you robbed of a soulful life,
Be your final resting friend?

Explain to me this,
Why we live in a shattered world?
Everyone is self obsessed and very cold.

My friend I convey this message of solitude,
I speak for those who never had a chance to,
I speak for those children buried alive,
Those who stare deeply into death's intense eyes
Those that never lived to see
The true wonder of life,
Those who were raped and brutally tortured
For just asking why!

Answer me this,
Why did I have to lose my life?
Why was I never given a choice?
For I know I would always say *no*
To the true horror of *war*.

Asha Abdi (12)
Sarah Bonnell School

Love Hurts When You're With Me

Love hurts when you're with me
I'll make you cry or I'll make you shout.

Love hurts when you're with me
I'll make you in pain and drive you mad.

Love hurts when you're with me
I'll make you beg so you don't leave
And I'll even make you make a tea.

Love hurts when you're with me
I'll make you sleep on the sofa
And tell all my friends a pack of lies
So they can jump and shout at you.

Love hurts when you're with me
I'll make you wash everything you see
Till your hands go all rotten.

Love hurts when you're with me
I'll make you start a painting of me
All day long till you go to sleep.

I'll tell you why, because I do something
Called cheat, that's what I do
That's why love hurts when you're with me.

So I told the truth so tell me yours
Does love hurt when I'm with you?
Tell me now before I cry!

Ifrah Abdi (12)
Sarah Bonnell School

Links

A red rose?
A satin heart?

No, I will give you a chain,
Its shining links will bind you
And link by link our love will grow.

The fine, flowing chain,
Will bind us together
And as we grow
And as our love grows,
So the chain will grow,
Thicken,
Strengthen.

The chain is our enemy,
The chain is our friend,
The chain is our prisoner -
Whose arms will join you to me.

But if you try to break from the irons of my love
The chain's cold grasp,
Will break
And you will be left standing bare and vulnerable.

So hold my gift close to you
And the warmth of your skin
Will melt the cold steel,
Just as you melted my heart.

Katherine Igoe-Ewer (12)
Sarah Bonnell School

Cousins

Cousins are so wonderful,
I'm glad that I know them,
As whom they are,
And that they are a part of me.

Cousins, big ones and small ones,
They're all equal to me,
They treat me and spoil me
And love me to bits.

Cousins, sisters and brothers,
They guide me day by day,
And keep me close,
That's why I love them so much.

They're always there for me,
When I'm down or sick at home,
They come and visit me
And help me through life.

When I'm stuck and trapped
And can't get out,
They show me a way
And free me from my misery.

They make me laugh,
Put a smile on my face.
When I've had a bad day
And nothing's gone right for me.

When I'm in darkness,
They show me light,
When I'm afraid,
They stand by my side.

So all I want to say to you all,
Is a big *thank you!*

Saera Sulthana (13)
Sarah Bonnell School

Me

Love, hate, feeling angry and sad,
All emotions I would love to escape.
I am what I am and that's how I be,
People never understand me, it's not that I don't try,
My only problem is I can never show what really matters to me,
Just because I don't smile doesn't mean I'm not happy,
Just because I don't laugh out doesn't mean I'm not laughing.
People that hate and hate on me,
I used to take offence to but not anymore.
Just because I'm quiet, shy and always looking depressed,
Doesn't mean I'm not here,
Feeling the same as you.
I'm trapped in this world feeling different emotions,
My business is my business and I keep it all to me,
People are so inner and they need to listen carefully,
Because I'm not gonna be here forever and neither are you,
I wanna make the most of my life and the best I can be,
I've grown into a person, person full of life,
I've grown to feel accepted, accepted because I'm me.
I'll always have different emotions, whether I like them or not,
I'll learn to get around them and be all that I can be.

Leila Douz (15)
Sarah Bonnell School

Rainbow

How do you make a rainbow?
Simple.
You just grab a blue ribbon,
Sparkling like the sea
Then plait some yellow string from the sun's rays.
After that pull some pink rope, soaked in happiness.
Finally put it all together
And spread over the sky
In an arch.

Artika Gunathasan (11)
Sarah Bonnell School

The School Rap

Here we go with the flow,
Slow, take it away
This is my school
It's so cool
With a big pool,
Er not for you!
For VIPs
We got some keys
It's not for males
And it ain't for sale
Now we got a pool
And it looks so cool.
Sarah Bonnell school
Always rules!

Marina Khan (11)
Sarah Bonnell School

Being Me

Throughout my life I've been everyone but me
I don't know if it's because I want to fit in
Or because I just need a change.
For fifteen years I've been with myself
And I still don't know what my favourite colour is
It seems as if I change myself at the blink of an eye.
I act differently in front of different people
And I'm still not part of *the group*.
One day I'll be who I'm meant to be
One day I'll find my personality
Or it'll find me
I don't care how it happens
I just want to be me.

Felicia Alamu (15)
Sarah Bonnell School

You're There

You're there . . .
I know
You're listening . . .
I know
You're a true friend . . .
I know
Because you're my special friend.

I'm crying . . .
You're there
I'm laughing . . .
You're there
I need help . .
You're there
I need advice . . .
You're there.

I'm confused . . .
You're there
I need support . . .
You're there.

You're there and always will be I know
But you must know I want to be the one
To be known to be there for you too.

Aisha Khan (15)
Sarah Bonnell School

Friends At War

I am the moon and you are the sun,
I am the tree and you are the bark,
I am the dark and you are the light,
I am the day and you are the night,
The star replied shining bright,
'You're more important than you'll ever know.'
I am the arrow and you are the bow,
With me you are weak,
With you I am strong,
With me life is short,
With you life is long.
The star then twinkled and told the two,
'You are both special, the world needs you.'

Natalie Ferguson (15)
Sarah Bonnell School

Feelings

Why do I keep being bad
and make everyone around me sad?

Why can't I be strong
and turn aside from doing wrong?

I want to be like a tree
and let no one influence me.

The tree is big and strong,
it doesn't do anything wrong.

I won't be like a tree,
but I need someone to help me.

Frankie Killick (13)
Spa Special School

Poem To Autumn

The season has begun,
the cold breezes have started to come,
the birds have started to sing,
even though it's nowhere near spring.

The poppies come in bunches,
oh! and those delicious lunches,
the flowers will have lots of bees,
surrounding them without any ease.

The mellowness of the fruit vines,
people will start to make lovely wines,
animals will get their sleep,
over the mountains and below steep.

The air has a wonderful smell,
indeed it smells oh so well,
autumn is on the way
and the children are still out at play.

Nicolette Nugent (13)
St Augustine's CE High School

My Hobbies

I love my warm, comforting bed
I also love the colour red.

I like watching TV
And buying lots of jewellery.

I love Justin Timberlake
Especially when I have a belly ache.

Another possession is my diary
No one's allowed to see except for me!

Ashani Solanki (11)
St Augustine's CE High School

Autumn In The City

Season of autumn in the city
So it is time to be ready for the winter
And in autumn the road in the city is so slippery
So be careful you little tinker!

In autumn the city is quite cold
So wake up to buy a new coat
But you are too bold
To buy them in a car boot!

In autumn the city is quite windy
And that is a dislike of the people
'Cause if it is windy it feels so lazy and lonely
And the wind is blowing you double.

In autumn the city is quite grumpy
And the people are so clumsy
'Cause the weather is always bumpy
And all over the place is really slummy.

And in the city people quite like autumn so much
'Cause you can sleep longer
And it is really good to sleep with a hunch
'Cause you can sleep really well curled up like a conger.

Joecris Aldea (12)
St Augustine's CE High School

September

September is the best,
Everyone knows it's true.
It's better than the rest
And brings the season blue.

It's better than November,
You think it's very new.
It's better than December
And October too.

Billy Garraghan (12)
St Augustine's CE High School

Ode To Autumn In The City

Autumn is when funny coloured leaves start falling off trees,
You see kids shivering with chattering teeth, walking off to school,
People using warm winter clothes, otherwise you'll hear the sound
of shaking knees,
People looking through windows of warm houses and their mouths
starting to drool,
Your teeth start to wobble whenever you feel a passing breeze,
You sit and watch how quickly the day flies by,
You look around and spot some hurtful looking conker shells,
Notice how autumn is becoming so cold and sly,
Up coming winter we're all getting ready to freeze,
But remember the blazing fire awaiting your arrival, so let your mind
rest and ease,
It seems like it's evening but only midday, you hear the ringing of
church bells.

Who knows what dreadful things winter has in store for all of us,
But if you watch carefully, you may find an answer.
Oh, be careful or you'll get drowned by a passing bus!
You feel autumn blow softly into your already wet hair,
You walk along and sniff the miserable-looking air,
On your way you pass children getting costumes ready for Hallowe'en.
You start to think about the sun shining on the other side of the world
And you say aloud, 'How unfair.'
You pass the once beautifully bright but now dying flowers,
It seems so strange how autumn seems so keen to keep things
muddy and unclean.
You sit down by a nearby tree and lean,
Watching autumn do his job incredibly lazily after hours and hours.

Finally, you get up and the day dies away,
Leaves brush past your muddy feet very swiftly.
Look up and see the setting winter sun shining off her last ray.
People are starting to pile up leaves in their gardens neatly,
Brrrrrrrr, your body shivers all the way down,
You hear autumn yawn and you start to frown.
Meanwhile, the city's getting extremely cold,
But remember, never forget the poem I told!

Habiba Ali (12)
St Augustine's CE High School

Ode To Autumn In The City

Leaves all around us once again,
as the cold mornings at the beginning of autumn
are coming around.

As the bloomed flowers begin to die
and the footsteps of people, step on the crunchy brown leaves,
that fall from the trees.

As people rush home from work in the late afternoon,
walking along the polluted streets
getting pushed and shoved trying to get home.

As the nights draw in and coldness comes along,
we say goodnight
now that summer has gone.

As we step out of our door into the chilly mornings,
we now know that autumn has come.

Sarah Sinclair (12)
St Augustine's CE High School

Autumn In The City

Autumn is the coldest and slyest season I've yet to meet,
Kids make no effort to wake in the morning, those little muppets,
To get their attention you need to tickle their feet,
Autumn is like a puppeteer and we are the puppets.

No matter how much you nag, you'll never get a single word out
of him,
Be sure to carry your first-aid kit with you, 'cause he'll make sure
you slip,

You'd better hurry, the night is getting dim,
If you're not steady he'll make you do a backward flip.

Autumn really wants to make trouble,
So make sure you keep an eye on him,
So keep your weapons ready at the double,
So stay out of trouble autumn or we'll tell big Kim.

Nadia Fadlymtiri (12)
St Augustine's CE High School

Autumn Is Autumn

Autumn gives out the wonderful breeze,
floating mildly amongst the trees,
Making the leaves go browner and browner,
off they fall, downer and downer.

Onto the ground they fall with no thud,
wrapping themselves with clots of mud.
Meeting new friends, twigs that are broken,
communicating, though none of them have spoken.

Staring into the light-blue sky,
watching all the birds fly by.
Looking down into the dried grass,
gazing as the insects scurry past.

Old grass, old leaves
and even old trees.
An old creation,
in an old nation.

In the city the church bell rings,
children playing on the swings.
The buzz of aeroplanes, the horns of cars,
there's autumn here, is it there in Mars?

There's soft grass, crunchy leaves,
dried up bark and rough trees.
It's time for autumn to go to another place,
to show its beauty in another space.

Autumn, autumn, you have been here,
I know you will come back next year.
Please, pretty please, do not die,
bye-bye autumn, bye-bye.

Rachael Adekunle (12)
St Augustine's CE High School

Autumn In The City

Longer, darker are the nights
Hazy glow beneath the lamp lights
Life goes on in the streets
Warmer footwear on your feet
Whistling winds that yell and bellow
Upturned collars on the fellows
Imprisoned beneath the city towers
Autumn waits and works its powers
Office blocks are dark and grey
People hurrying on their way
The world is full of doom and gloom
Waiting for summer's bloom
The rain comes down in short, sharp showers
Frost settles on the flowers
But autumn has another side
One that we simply cannot hide
So what secrets does autumn hold?
A season rich with red, amber, gold
Autumn has such wonderful sights
And fills us with great delight
Crispy crunching on the ground
Autumn has such wondrous sounds
Autumn is not bad at all
In America they call it 'the fall'
Autumn is a clever season
Why say this? I have good reason
Out with the old, in with the new
Waiting for winter right on cue
Although my explanation has been told
It has a story to behold.

Charles Whittock (12)
St Augustine's CE High School

The Sense Of Autumn

Autumn is the season of fall,
All the trees grow leafless and bold,
School children are stamping across the streets,
You could hear the crispy leaves crunch,
As they hurry to get to school.

In autumn animals go into hibernation,
Some animals stay awake,
Listening to cars, feeling the wind,
All nice and cosy in their fur skins,
At home you could sit down and rest.

The thing I hate about autumn,
Is the cold, the wet and the grey mornings,
The nights too long, the days too short,
The nights don't seem to end,
But remember, winter is around the bend.

Autumn is a killer of many things,
But it still gives life to many,
It kills all the flowers,
But it gives us fruit, nuts and berries,
Oh, it's a lovely season to have!

Amzod Ali (13)
St Augustine's CE High School

Ode To Autumn In The City

Fallen allies on the yellow grass,
Shot down by the swift winnowing wind,
There are little soldiers left on their base,
For the soldiers their lives have dimmed.

Why has this suddenly occurred?
Because the season of death has come.
Juicy apples, darker days
And in the south the hummingbirds hum.

Rain and wind stronger than ever,
Whilst insects fight for their lives,
People will fight with the wind with umbrellas,
While bees try to get to their hives.

Naked trees on the streets,
Trying to scratch the window,
Some conkers crack on the ground,
While some of the others still grow.

Autumn is nearly over,
There's the last sigh of the wind,
The last raindrops touch the ground,
Here come the songs of winter.

Vay Soen Ly (12)
St Augustine's CE High School

Autumn

The rough wind blows so hard,
It looks like the trees are going mad,
The trees begin to sing,
Like they have just been crowned by their king.

The squirrels prepare to hibernate,
Because this is going to be a very long date,
The insects begin to cry
Because they will soon die.

The sun goes down in shame,
But face it, he's not to blame,
The rain comes down to flood,
Now that he's the new god.

This produces honey
As easy as a rabbit will produce a bunny.
This produces vines
So people can have a taste of wine.

Abayomi Badejoko (12)
St Augustine's CE High School

My Poem

Stars, stars everywhere,
When I look it makes me glare.
Water, water pour on me,
That will be the special key!
Sea, sea all around here
And there from top to ground.
Sunshine, sunshine shine on me,
When I'm having a cup of tea!
Family, family that's all I want,
Even more than a sweet little dove.

Sheren Mhanaya (11)
St Augustine's CE High School

Mankind

The Earth,
A place masked
Masked with pretence, intent on ruefulness,
And plagued with pride.

Women fight over men,
Men fight over women.
We prowl for attention, so we can be envied,
But hate to be the ones who are envious.

Politicians stress the importance of the law,
Yet when they, or their family are in trouble,
They manage to twist and manipulate the rules.
Should action not be taken?
Or should we just sweep it under the carpet?

People who should live for today,
Dwell on the past.
We punish ourselves with regret,
Thinking that some way the situation will improve.

We have a disease, a disease of smugness.
We look down on people,
People we think we are greater than.
Open up your eyes, my friends and look in the mirror,
For underneath our masks, we are all the same.

Kaladerhan Agbontaen (12)
St Augustine's CE High School

Autumn's Spark

Autumn is the spark in the trees,
animals hibernating, including the bees.
Green, yellow, red and brown,
the colours of the leaves dropping in the town.

Lorries, vans, cars that beep,
adults, children, babies that sleep.
People walking on the street,
stamping leaves with their feet.

People knocking on the church door,
bringing food at harvest for the poor.
People singing, the church bell rings,
snow-white doves flapping their wings.

Broken twigs are on the ground,
little insects running around.
Looking for a place to rest,
rabbits in burrows, birds in nests.

Autumn is a wonderful season,
beautiful flowers do please 'em.
We are so happy autumn is here,
now we will wait till it comes next year.

Melisa Da Costa (12)
St Augustine's CE High School

Shipwreck Of The Turbulent Sea

Cool, calm, collected, the ship set off slowly on its voyage,
Destined for the exotic, mystical lands of the great Earth.
Willing explorers enthusiastically got aboard
With great expectations of future discoveries,
Absorbed in the vistas of the oceans,
Relaxed by the cold but refreshing breeze pressing against the masts.
Passengers enjoyed the dazzling waters, gazed at their reflections;
Their skins shimmered in the sun's gold, vibrant light.
At ease, many drifted into dreams and deep sleep,
Reassured by the flawless conditions on which they were resting.

Suddenly, an abrupt and startling tempest sprang from the torrential
seas.
Gust and gale seethed, spluttered and spattered swiftly from inky,
jet-black clouds.
Frail and tender like a flower's petal, the vessel rocked, tossed and
turned.
Then alas, it plunged between two roaring walls of water, then
cracked and split!
Its cargo of wailing, shrieking souls were flung around,
Dependent upon the boisterous waves, unprotected by the former
ship.
Survivors clung with sheer desperation to the shattered wreck,
Until its remnants washed onto the shore
With corpses and relics of the disaster -

The only proof of its existence.

Sarah Galal (16)
The London Oratory School

Hybrid Heart

a lone, shrivelled heart recalls
unforgotten darkness,
unforgotten dread.
unlocked from time - unearthed
a whispered story of moments and distance.
entwined,
in wait.

one is created, a whole
an autumn of formalities -
a familiar stranger
interlinked, yet so distant.
two steps closer.
a network of cold provocation
so sudden - untruthful.
the sound of breathing,
a soul possessed.

the heat is on the edge
unloved and alone
touched but never held.

eras build walls and some measure of strength
denial is convicted
and the truth -
presented to me as a hybrid heart.
a disadvantage? possibly.
the curtains fall,
and the actors rise . . .
facing each other, facing the truth.

coffee keeps the heart pumping
the wound is sealed . . . for now.

Amna Ahmad (16)
The Mount School

Midst Of Night

In the midst of night
The land grew dark
At the midsummer field
That is larger than the park

The air is freezing
A chill ran down my spine
Though the night is cold
It will pass the time

A group of lights
They all come and go
They are fireflies
Calm and slow

Few night animals
Appear at night
What are they?
Dear moon shine your light

The moon has shone
Its beautiful light
Now we see
The animals at night

The wise hoot of the owl
The black flight of bats
The smooth sly of the fox
The calm prowl of the wildcats

O lovely moon
And its beauty star
You will shine your light
Near yet so far

O beautiful sight
O wonderful silvery light
This is the mysterious life
Of the midst of night.

Louise De Spon (16)
The Whitefield Special School & Centre

Don't

Don't wet the bed
Don't watch horror films
Don't punch girls
I don't like trifle
Don't say rude names
I don't like Sky movies
I like Tom and Jerry
We like Pizza Hut
I like cats.

Jamie Stansfield (13) & Babak Mashoof (14)
The Whitefield Special School & Centre

Wedding

W earing a ring
E ating a fruit cake
D oing a dance
D oing a toast
I love you
N ice wedding dress
G oing on honeymoon.

Henry Ekeke (16)
The Whitefield Special School & Centre

Don't

Don't put the drain in the plane
Don't give a shark a bit of bark for its birthday
Don't play with that gun, it's not fun
Don't be naughty, you're forty!

Andrew Clarke (12)
The Whitefield Special School & Centre

Life Doesn't Frighten Me At All

Loud bangs in the night
Bright lights give me a fright
Party poppers in my ear
Bangers make me sweat with fear
Nasty sick gushing and I go away
rushing.
Roller coasters flying high
Twisting and turning in the sky
Makes me scream, 'I'm going to die!'
Balloons pop loud
Makes me feel bowed
But running away keeps me lucky!
These things only happen
Once in a while
So, see me smile.

Jesse Mensah (13)
The Whitefield Special School & Centre